THE ART OF DYING

Robert E. Neale

THE
ART OF DYING

HARPER & ROW, PUBLISHERS
New York • Evanston • San Francisco • London

Library of Congress Cataloging in Publication Data

Neale, Robert E
    The art of dying.
    Bibliography: p.
    1. Death. I. Title.
BT825.N4   1973   128'.5   72–11361
ISBN 0–06–066090–2

To Margo

CONTENTS

REBIRTH

Preface

"In the midst of life we are in death." To live is to wonder about life. And life includes death and dying. So it has been said that "death is a truth made profound by the size of our wonder." Unfortunately, our wonder about death tends to be pitifully minute. Full wonder would engender a process of death, gestation, and rebirth. In the midst of death we can be in life.

The purpose of these exercises is to facilitate our own movement from death to life. In the section on death, we will explore our awareness of death in the midst of life and our fear of death and life. By such contemplation we may die a little. In the section on gestation, we will explore our living death in life and the possibility of our transformation by grief. Hopefully, we will gestate. And in the final section on rebirth, we will explore our beliefs concerning life in death and our awareness of the delights of living in the midst of death. If movement occurs, we will live a little more deeply than before. The exercises do require a descent. Our path leads directly to the chaotic hell of our own denial of death, fear of life, and suicidal living. There can be no rebirth without a death. But after the descent, there is an ascent into our own grief, beliefs, and joy in the midst of life and death. Through death we are granted the possibility of rebirth in this life. Although the focus of the exercises is our own death, the intent is exploration of our own living.

I cannot write about human death without benefit of personal pronouns. A human death is my death or your death or the death of a loved one, not just a death. The exercises are a product of my own wonder about seeing a newborn baby lying in his casket, waiting with families as they watched their children die, holding hands with numerous people while they died, and being with my brother who died after five years of illness. The exercises are also the result of experiences in seminars and workshops over the past decade with hundreds of people of all ages, backgrounds, and vocations. They have shaped the material as much as I have. In the course of typing the manuscript, Suzanne Locklair has contributed provocative editing. Clarence Collins, my colleague and friend, has exposed me to the responses of the health professions. Cecily Saunders and Barbara McNulty have watched over me as I watched with the dying. And my wife, to whom these exercises are dedicated, has helped me experience and understand the death, gestation, and rebirth that I have been talking about all these years. It is the movement of these people, both the living and the dead, that has created what wonder I can express.

The important question now concerns your own wonder. The exercises are constructed to help you explore yourself. Mechanically all you need bring to them are pencil and paper. But no exercise is self-working. I hope you will not read all the exercises in one evening, seek only information and opinion from the authorities, or reflect only on the dying and living of others. To do so would severely limit the possibility of genuine wonder. Rather you should do one exercise a week in the company of one or more persons. Taking time, reflecting on yourself and sharing with others, will help the process rule over the content.

The time to begin exploration is now, before you participate in the first exercise. Take pencil and paper and write at the top of the sheet, "My Own Death." Write a statement of no more than fifty words on the subject. Do not worry about spelling, grammar, or literary merit. Do not worry about what is the

right thing to say. Worry about whether you can wonder about
your own death. Then write fifty words. Do it now before reading any further.

Having taken this first step, you might be interested in what
others have said. Here is a sampling. Remember that they are
not to be judged right or wrong any more than your statement
is.

Death for me, at this point, brings scattered thoughts; each one torn
with emotion. Emotion is the only thing that unites them. Fear to the
point of panic when I think of my own death. Emptiness and pain
crying out when I think of the deaths of those I have loved. Helplessness and a need to give when I remember patients who died—especially those who still clung to life.

The thought of my own death brings up nothing, just a void. Death
gives me the impression of overwhelming absence; absence of pain,
absence of growing. My own death still seems impossible.

Death is a natural process as the human body is made up of organisms
which can last only a certain length of time. It is. . . .

A very threatening way to begin the exercises! Not because death is
threatening but probably because one's relation to it is so deep inside.
Can that be revealed—even anonymously? Can that even be known?

Pain—fear—hurt.
The end—no more chances—no more potential—no more possibilities.
No more regrets—no more hate—no more love.
No more yes—no more chance for yes.
No more bells, no more time for mine to ring.
Does the end sanctify the beginning?
Or did the beginning absolutize the end?
Will anyone know I was ever here?
How can you say yes to that no?

I don't so much fear my own death or even the process of dying. The
reason I fear thinking about death is that immediately it gets me
thinking and feeling about how I'm *living*—how I have potential

which I don't fulfill, how little I deeply love, how I often just don't realize that I'm living and what it means. It gets me thinking about my mortality—I don't have forever to live.

I welcome it as the door to freedom from time, space, and individuality. What may be in the future I can't know and about it I'm not concerned. Life has been for me good—rewarding. Since I would not have it continue indefinitely I can welcome its end.

After reading these statements, read your own again. Ask yourself about the unexpected. What surprises you about the statements you read? What surprises you about your own statement? And what surprises you about the process of making such a statement? Such surprises are perfect occasions for learning. Hopefully, they will occur during each exercise.

ROBERT E. NEALE

DEATH

In the Midst of Life

To begin at the beginning is to acknowledge the difficulty of the task. The theme of this exercise is that we do not want to do what we are about to do. Three questions will be developed: Do we make too much or too little of death? Is it possible to become aware of our own death? Is it useful to become aware of our own death? The dynamics to be explored are revealed by the statement a man once made to his wife: "If one of us dies, I'll go to Paris."

Intimacy with Death

What would it have been like to experience dying and death a hundred years ago in a small rural community? When someone was dying, everyone would know it, even the children. The dying man would be in his home, attended by his family. Many would visit him. At the very moment of death his family, including children, and friends would be present. They would often hear from and speak last words to the dying, and then observe the cessation of breathing, relaxation of the body, and loss of skin color. The members of the family would prepare the corpse for last rites and the burial. Most of the community would attend these rites. In a small village, the bell does toll for everyone. Any death upsets the balance of community life, and the attempt to restore harmony begins with the funeral. It is the community that sees the body, carries it to the grave, and buries it. So in a village this final crisis of man is known intimately by everyone. There is no easy escape from consciousness of death.

The contemporary urban situation is quite different. Certainly death is all about us, perhaps even more than before. The news of the day is news of death. A newspaper is an obituary column writ large, containing reports of death by automobile accident, heart attack and cancer, suicide, murder, famine, flood, fire, and war. Death surrounds us, yet we are not so intimate with it as before. The dying are now to be found in hospitals, not visited at all by casual acquaintances and only occasionally by friends. The final moments of life are rarely observed even by the family. (Have you been present at the death of someone you loved?) Then the body disappears, not to a church for the whole community, but to a funeral home for family and selected friends. Attendance at the burial is even smaller. And we no longer see earth thrown back into the hole, let alone do it ourselves. Finally, such things as laying out great meals for all who attend the rites, holding a wake, or employing a Dixieland band are passing out of popular custom. All this means that the community has been separated from the dying and the dead. Death is all around us, but circumstances do not provide the intimacy which until quite recent times has been universal.

Take a moment now to reflect on your own intimacy with death. Answer the following questions and then share them with others. What were the circumstances that encouraged and discouraged exposure to death?

1. Have you ever seen an embalmed body?   Yes____ No____
2. Have you ever seen an *un*embalmed body?   Yes____ No____
3. Have you ever seen a person die?   Yes____ No____
4. How often have you been in a situation in which you seriously thought you might die?   Never   ____

Once or twice   ____
Several times   ____
Many times   ____

5. When has a member of your family, a close relative, or a
   very close friend died?   Within past year   ____
                                        Within past two years ____
                                        Within past five years ____
                                        Over five years ago   ____
                                        Never   ____

6. Is a member of your family, a close relative, or a very close
   friend dying of an illness at the present time?   Yes____ No____

7. When did you last attend a funeral or memorial service?
                                        Within past year   ____
                                        Within past two years ____
                                        Within past five years ____
                                        Over five years ago   ____
                                        Never   ____

8. When you were a child, how was death talked about in
   your family?   Openly   ____
                                        Guardedly   ____
                                        With exclusion of children

                                                              ____
                                        Not talked about   ____
                                        Cannot remember   ____

Our lack of real intimacy with death is not irrevocably bad.
But it can lead to making too much or too little of death. Of
course, such tendencies are not new, but the contemporary
situation may foster extreme reactions.

Consider a dead body and our response to it. It is hard to
consider! Artists find it most difficult to portray a corpse. Look
at paintings and you will see that the body usually seems alive
—it is asleep or on a journey. The many dead Christs are not
dead but are suffering (which no actual corpse does) or are
waiting (which no actual corpse does) for the resurrection.
Leonard Baskin is one of the rare artists who has actually pic-
tured dead men. He sculptured bodies that are so without signs

of life that they are most difficult to respond to. We are accustomed to responding to life, even in situations where there is none—in corpses. On the surface at least, many people simply do not react at all to Baskin's creatures. This lack of response is a sign that the artist has succeeded. Naturally such success does not lead to public acclaim! The artist and his work are nothing. A corpse is nothing—that which evokes no response. In this case, we may be making too little of death.

A visit to an autopsy by a layman usually evokes the opposite response. You walk into a room containing many tables. On most of them are dead bodies of all shapes, sizes, and colors. It is a scene appropriate for color television, for the innards of a corpse are rich in color. The usual hospital smell is heightened and modified as the medical examiner opens the bowels. It is uncanny to see a face peeled off and back over the skull as if a mask were being removed. For the inexperienced layman these perceptions evoke powerful reactions. For days afterward the images remain lurking and springing up into consciousness unexpectedly. They tend to rule over all perceptions of life. In this case, we may be making too much of death.

And now consider your own corpse. Can you do so? As an aid, imagine what is done to your body by an undertaker. Or, look in a mirror and imagine the face you see as it would appear when dead. Can you do it? If you actually can, how do you respond?

This experiment raises the question of appropriate reactions. Is it making too little of death to dismiss such meditation as morbid? Is it making too much of death to dwell on what happens once in a lifetime and may well be an inaccessible experience anyway? Is there really any way to make such evaluations, since the needs of individuals vary so greatly and are so difficult to decipher? Take your own preliminary stand right now by answering the following questions.

1. How often do you think about the possibility of your own
   death?   Never   ____
            Seldom (once a year or less)   ____
            Now and then   ____
            Frequently   ____
            Very often (once a day or more)   ____
2. Do you think you make too much or too little of your own
   death?   Too much   ____
            Too little   ____
            Neither   ____

These questions are not purely academic. We answer them
every day and behave on the basis of our answers. This occurs
most obviously when we debate the appropriate nature of last
rites. There are relatives who display the corpse for viewing,
make it a visible part of the funeral service, accompany it to the
cemetary, and watch it being lowered into the ground. Are they
making too much of death? Or consider the increasing contemporary practice of immediate cremation upon death. In this
process the corpse plays absolutely no part at all. Are the people
who plan in advance to have such last rites making too little of
death?

We all have answers to these questions about funeral practices. The answers reflect our values, which are the result of
innumerable factors. Does anyone have the right answers? I
do of course. And so do you. Or to put it another way, there
are no right answers, no revelations from on high to be legis-
lated for all individuals in society. So beware of two things:
(1) assuming that we have no answers and are totally
unbiased, and (2) assuming that we have *the* answer and are
totally right.

It may well be that some of us make too little of death
while others make too much of it. The problem is that we are
quite unable to distinguish between them in any concrete
case.

Possibility of Awareness

The issue of intimacy and the question of making too much or too little of death lead to another consideration. Is it even possible to become aware of one's own death? Maurice Maeterlinck proclaimed, "There is only one event, in our life and in our universe, that really counts, and this is death." Is such a statement really possible? Is it existentially possible to say as so many have, that to be alive is to know that one has to die? One out of one dies. Yes, but we affirm that statistics lie. So one out of one dies—with one exception: me. Let us look at some of our ways of denying death. There are as many ways as there are human beings; we are all masters at the art. But there are three obvious methods we adopt.

The first method is to simply ignore death in toto. A classic example is the traditional policy of the *Christian Science Monitor*, which did not permit use of the term "death." The modern life-insurance salesman does not ask, "How will your family be taken care of if you should die tomorrow?" Rather he is instructed to say, "How would your family be taken care of if you had died yesterday?" "If I should die tomorrow" give rise to fears which do not help the salesman, whereas "If I had died yesterday" offers a comfortable impossibility. How this method of denial clashes with the harsh words of scripture: "Fool! This night your soul is required of you." Our first reaction to death is to ignore it totally if at all possible.

In the second method we do not altogether ignore death, but deny its harshness. Our inventiveness in this respect is dazzling to behold. Death is denied by all the euphemisms we use; we do not die nowadays, we "expire," "depart," "pass away," or "pass on;" sometimes we just "sleep." We do not fill in a death certificate, but complete a "vital statistics form." We are not advised to buy a grave, but to "invest in a pre-need memorial estate." We attempt to preserve and prettify the corpse, trying to create the illusion of life or at least momentary sleep, and we customarily observe to the bereaved that this painted corpse looks "very natural." Our language and our actions on the occasion of death bespeak our need to deny its harshness.

The third common method of denying death is more subtle and even seems to refute the idea that we strive to deny it. Our society seems preoccupied with death. Some newspapers maintain a large circulation by vivid portrayal of violent death. Westerns, detective stories, and spy novels achieve mass circulation by the inclusion of numerous and detailed presentations of death. According to Marc Golden, formerly in charge of program development at CBS:

There's one constant in every successful dramatic TV story form, and that's that the leading character's occupation is somehow connected with death. We've tried stories about publicity men, Congressmen, social workers. They've all been unsuccessful. I don't know why, but story forms connected with death are the only ones that home audiences are willing to watch in numbers large enough to make a dramatic series economically viable.[1]

Why do we delight in these death-dealing adventures? According to social anthropologist Geoffrey Gorer our fascination is pornographic.[2]

This word, connected by definition with the obscene—i.e., what is "offensive to taste . . . loathsome; disgusting"— has always been associated with sexuality. Pornography refers to those writings, photographs, and works of art created to excite us sexually and give rise to private sexual fantasies. A breast or penis is presented as an object. Even presentation of a whole body is not made or responded to as a person. The private fantasies can be nothing but doing something to an object, each fantasy becoming more complicated or sensational than the last. What is sexual pornography? It is a way of fulfilling a sexual need without being involved with another person. It occurs when a society is prudish. When society says that sex is disgusting or immoral and not to be talked about, sexual need is not destroyed but only forced into unhuman paths. And pornographic preoccupations may rule in any individual who lacks sufficient trust to relate to another human being.

The "pornography" of death follows the same pattern. Mass media make little bid for our normal feelings of sorrow, guilt, and love at the occasion of death. The creators of Mike Hammer and James Bond seemed only to be making each successive novel contain more spectacular ways of dying. And our response contains no more genuine human feelings than that of the collector of filthy pictures. So death not only surrounds us in our time, but we search it out. We seek it in order to deny it. We do not deny death in toto, and we do not deny death's harshness in this case. Rather, we emphasize the harshness and deny our tenderness. This occurs partially because our society is prudish about death, sees it as disgusting, immoral, and not to be talked about. Yet since there is a fundamental need to come to terms with all elements of life, including dying and death, the end result is pornographic perversion. And we may be ruled by this perversion insofar as we lack sufficient trust to relate to life. In the attempt to ignore death, we are led to morbid preoccupation with bizarre fantasies which successfully keep us from a humane response.

These three common methods of denial may not have touched on your particular genius. Indeed, I have not mentioned mine. I have four ways that I know about. First, I put the focus on my family, relatives, and community rather than on myself. In his provocative essay "The Concept of Death," Franz Borkenau finds that cultures can be characterized as death-denying, death-defying, or death-accepting.[3] The latter characterization is applied to the Judeo-Hellenic cultures, in which imagery of and concern about afterlife is minimal. The focus is on the community, the survivors who remember and extol the glory of the Greek hero or the survivors who will participate in the future glory of the community of Israel. For Borkenau, the playing down of the individual death and stress of future generations is acceptance of death. But is minimizing one's own death actually acceptance of it? And when I reflect, as so many do, that my death will be less tragic for me than for the survivors, am I really perceiving and accepting my own death? I doubt it. It seems more likely that I am refusing to look at it.

The second way I deny death is used by terminal patients. Those who are going to get well tend to assume that they are going to recover sooner than is the case. Patients who are dying tend to assume that death will occur far later than is really the case.[4] What I do is say to myself, "Sure I'm going to die, but not for a long, long time."

A third thing I do is to visit the dying in a professional setting. Once I spent six months doing this. Why? In some part, no doubt, so I could say to myself: "I am not like them. They are dying, but I'm living," and "They are dead, but I'm alive." Work with the dying has many aspects; some are not without irony.

Finally, I am trying to deny death in writing these exercises. When I first began to gather material, I became very depressed. Some of you may become so while reading. Then the depression lifted, as it will lift for you. But why? In part because you will believe, as I do, that you are now one up on death because of these cute exercises and intellectual niceties. We will learn in order to control what cannot be controlled.

These are four out of the undoubtedly many arrangements I make to deny death. What do you do? I suspect you are as talented as I am. Much, if not most, of what we do with death suggests that we flee awareness.

In what way do you tend to deny death? Check only one of the following:

I do not deny death   ____

I deny death totally   ____

I deny the harshness of death   ____

I deny the humane aspects of death   ____
Other (use only a word or two)   _____

If it is true that we are no longer in intimate contact with death and tend to deny death, what can we do? Some have reasoned that we should turn to those who still have contact—medical men and clergymen.

We believe that doctors know a great deal about dying and death. Most of their time is spent with people who face the prospect of death and do die in their presence. But doctors are human beings who seek to deny death as we do, and they live under conditions which foster this goal.

Traditionally, a student begins his study of medicine with a cadaver. He probes and analyzes the blood, bones, and organs on a dissecting table. He is trained as an expert in diagnosis and treatment of diseased bodies. This traditional orientation in medical training has positive results, but also two negative effects. The first concerns fear of death. Such symbols of death as blood, bones, corpses, and the stench of the dead no longer have meaning after a few years of training. The doctor has conquered his fear of the fate of the body. But the fear of death is more than this, and the doctor is liable to be unaware of the fears that still motivate his behavior. He does not have the self-awareness we might expect.

The second negative effect of this training concerns his objectivity. A cadaver is different from a live body, even one that is dying. The doctor is trained to work with bodies; very rarely is he trained to work with people, to understand and aid a personality. Medical school discussions on the dynamics of the dying are almost always limited to ways to get permission for surgery and autopsy. So it is understandable that a doctor frequently becomes extremely uncomfortable in the presence of a dying patient and retreats to his habitual clinical objectivity. Curiosity about a corpse does not lead to intimacy with dying.

The other condition that fosters denial in the doctor is the very goal of medicine. An old children's verse goes: "Doctor, Doctor, will I die / Yes, my child, and so will I." Here is the ultimate challenge to the profession. The goal of medicine is the *promotion of life*. This goal is commonly interpreted as the *prolongation of life*. Death is the archenemy of doctors. But the goal is never reached; the enemy always wins. It would not be pleasant to spend the whole of one's professional life waging a losing battle. When a doctor visits his dying patient, he faces his own helplessness. The confession of a psychiatrist reveals this reaction. He writes:

I will . . . mention the ungrateful affrontery of one who dies despite our most skillful ministrations, the narcissistic damage to a vaunted intellect proved ignorant, the deep wounds to omnipotence when we are shown to be quite impotent. In addition, we are busily denying death, and here is a person doing his level best to demonstrate its reality. I submit that it is no wonder psychiatrists say little can be done with dying patients; it is true, but I suspect it is not the fault of the dying patient.[5]

If this is the predicament of the doctor, many things become understandable. We know why there are so few lectures or discussions in medical school on the care of the dying. We know why doctors tend to be objective, distant, even harsh in the presence of the dying. We know why they visit these patients so rarely and briefly. We know why they have the tradition of hiding the truth from a patient and offering what is frequently destructive reassurance. The goal of negating death leads to denial of its presence.

Another professional group which has close contact with dying and death is the clergy. The minister visits the dying patient and his family. He helps the family in many practical matters at the time of death. Her officiates at the last rites. And he comforts the bereaved for some time after the death. By nature of his profession, the minister is thrust even more than the doctor into the midst of death. But ministers are also human beings who seek to deny death, and they live under special conditions which foster this goal.

In discussing the minister, we ought to first look at his chief concern: religion. Some have said that religion is born of fear. A few have been even more specific and claimed that it is born out of fear of death. This is not the whole story by any means, but there is some truth in it. Later in these exercises we shall see how these beliefs serve men well—to do so here would be premature. For according to the Judeo-Christian tradition, we are all sinners. Therefore we misuse the gifts we have received. The greatest of all these gifts is our faith, and this is what we may misuse the most. We use our faith against God and against life, especially that part of life we call dying. To sin and play god is to remove oneself from contingencies of finite life. What could suit our purposes more than to promote doctrines of immortality and resurrection? There is no greater tool for the denial of death and dying than religious belief.

The minister has greater occasion and need for this tool than anyone else. He is called into the presence of the dying and bereaved who seek his ultimate reassurance. He represents the divine, and yet he is only another human being. He is asked about mysteries which are as mysterious to him as to all others. He is expected to speak convincingly about eternal life, but is fearful about his own mortality. He is bombarded with desperate cries of "Why—why—why!!?"—and he does not know why. The minister's predicament in the face of death is extreme. The demands placed upon him are more than he can bear. And the strength and guidance of the Holy Spirit does not always seem to be present.

Under these stressful conditions, the minister flees intimacy with dying and death. He does this very easily. He reassures the dying patient and the bereaved survivors with all the tools at his disposal. As soon as he suspects that people are going to open themselves to him with all their suffering, he cuts them off with

"The Lord is my shepherd" or "Let us pray." Scripture and prayer are used by the anxious minister to shut people up and shut them out of his presence. Such reassurance for the patient is premature and its basic purpose is to reassure the minister himself. He may spend much time with the dying and bereaved; he is a very busy man, always around, always doing something helpful. This may look good, but the busyness is frequently a way of avoiding the problems surrounding death. During a funeral the minister will be circumspect about death according to the standards of "good taste." Once when I was younger and a little bit more foolish than now, I spoke of death during a funeral, saying, "This man lying in this casket is dead." As you may guess, the statement caused no end of consternation. It was a foolish thing to do for several reasons, but it is striking that although the scripture read at funerals speaks clearly and boldly of death, it is not considered proper for the minister to do so in modern English. At the one time when death is most obvious to a Christian community, the Church flees into dogmas of eternal life. That little item in between life and eternity gets lost.

To see all medical men and clergymen as authorities on death and dying would be a mistake. Some are deeply related to their fellowmen and to God. But many have been poorly trained, have been pushed toward death too frequently and too harshly, and have developed a professional need to deny. These comments are not made to disparage their respective professions. Rather they should serve as a warning to you about these exercises. As a resource person in both psychiatry and religion, I may have a stronger need to deny death than you do. Your thoughts and feelings may well be more sound than mine or those of the professionals I quote. You are well advised to argue with the contents of the exercises all you can. But if I am right to some degree, than the whole enterprise in which we are engaged is quite presumptous! Some have believed such an attempt to be impossible. La Rochefoucauld asserted that "one cannot look directly at either the sun or death." Sigmund Freud concluded:

Our own death is indeed unimaginable and whenever we make an attempt to imagine it we can perceive that we really survive as spectators. Hence, the psychoanalytic school could venture the assertion that at bottom no one believes in his own death, or to put the same thing in another way, in the unconscious every one of us is convinced of his own immortality.[6]

So we not only have the desire to deny the fact of our own death, but may be unable to do otherwise. Much of the evidence would seem to be against our enterprise. But this is how every pilgrim begins his path, with the knowledge of the difficulty and even the impossibility of his venture.

Usefulness of Awareness

Supposing for a moment that we can become aware of our own death, is such awareness useful? To approach this question some understanding of "awareness" is necessary. In the course of conducting a sociological examination of interaction of patients and hospital staff in a number of institutions in California, Barney Glaser and Anselm Strauss created a typology of "awareness contexts."[7] I shall summarize these without final judgment as to which pattern is preferable. At least, I hope I can do this. And I hope you can receive them in the same way. Of course if we are unsuccessful in this attempt, we learn something about ourselves—the amount of anxiety within us.

One context which occurs between patient and staff is called "closed awareness." The patient does not know that he is going to die. The physician in charge decides to keep the patient from knowing or even suspecting what the diagnosis actually is. He and the rest of the staff do all they can to maintain the patient's lack of knowledge and unsuspecting awareness. In this they take on a large task. The patient wants to know at least something about his future. Can he trust the staff? The staff wants his trust. Therefore they must do two things: *both* create a fictional story of the patient's future and get and keep his trust. No small feat!

There are many possible consequences for the patients. I once assumed that dying patients in a hospital cannot support each other. But they can. They can support each other's closed awareness and each other's hopes. I recall two men near death, each trying to get better. One moved to a different hospital. Having been friends in their first setting they corresponded with one another, and one actually made special and difficult arrangements to visit the other. Even when one of them died, the other "knew" that the hopes of the deceased still supported him. Patients can carry on their work as usual, converting their hospital bed to an office. They can continue their family relationships in a nearly normal manner. They are likely to be quite cooperative with the staff in the belief that by doing so they will be returned to good health. But they may shorten their lives because they do not realize what is required for prolonging their survival. And they cannot plan realistically for their families' future.

After considering the context of closed awareness, we conclude that there are many consequences, that it is not easy to predict them in advance, and that it is quite difficult to evaluate them even after they occur.

The next context Glaser and Strauss discuss is that of "suspicion awareness." The patient is neither ignorant nor aware of the true circumstances, but somewhere between the two. He suspects that he is going to die but does not know for sure. What happens when the staff knows, but conceals, and the patient suspects? The most common event is a contest, a contest for the control of information. The patient desires confirmation of his suspicion. He needs evidence, and so must either *detect* or *elicit* signs that will confirm his suspicions. It is a case of one man against a highly organized and experienced team. He has no allies. He may be immobile. He has few resources. And he must outwit the countertactics of the enemy. So the patient may peek at his medical charts or try to overhear staff discussions. He may ask a direct question: "Will I die?" He does not hope for a direct, honest answer, but for clues which appear when the staff is caught off guard. Or he may just proclaim that he is dying and gauge the reactions. I recall a woman who at the beginning of our first meeting said, "I'm dying." She looked right at me, in me, and through me. I felt caught off guard (it is interesting that we assume that we have to be "on guard"). The problem is that the patient still has the task of interpretation. Even the most systematic assessment of many clues rarely settles the issue with finality.

The tactics of the staff are basically the same as in the closed awareness situation. But the suspicious situation is more difficult, so the staff is likely to indicate to the patient how he is to behave. Directly or indirectly, he is told that he is overstepping his rights. As the story goes, a patient once died and went to heaven but was not certain where he was. He asked a nurse nearby: "Am I dead?" She responded: "Have you asked your doctor?" The patient's claim is met by a counterclaim. He is told that he is out of order.

What are the consequences? The patient may be lulled into belief that his suspicions are unfounded, so that the consequences are the same as for a patient with closed awareness. Or one who maintains his suspicions without confirmation may experience all these same consequences, perhaps with some additional cautionary measures such as drawing up a will "just in case." But the important thing to realize is that suspicion awareness is highly unstable. The patient usually oscillates between more and less suspicion. His spirits go up and down. He may even convert to another type of awareness.

The comments of Glaser and Strauss are most negative on this context. I am inclined to agree. But this awareness can be changed to closed awareness, which has some benefits to all concerned. And it is certainly possible that suspicion awareness is better than some possible results of confirming the suspicion. I recall a burly, intelligent policeman who angrily accused the doctors of concealing his diagnosis from him. They had not done so. I arranged that he would be carefully told again. He again refused to hear. He wanted to know and he did not want to know. He was angry, very angry. The anger was a response to his anxiety. So suspicion ruled, and the staff made no further attempts to eliminate it. The suspicion was serving a useful purpose—for the time being. At a later stage in his living and dying, he did seek to hear his diagnosis and accepted it. But for many months this was not an appropriate avenue for him. Even with regard to suspicion awareness, we should avoid snap judgments.

The third type of awareness context is the "ritual drama of mutual pretense." This occurs when both patient and staff know that the patient is dying and both agree to act *as if* he were going to live. The researchers characterize the interaction as a *masquerade*. It is an informal drama in which the script is written as the play proceeds. There is an extensive use of props. Masks: these hide the facial expressions which are appropriate to the real situation. Costumes: patients dress for the part of not-dying, paying special attention to good grooming. Stage sets: fixing up the room so it is just like home. Both the patient and the staff cooperate in the use of these props to maintain the pretense. But maintenance is not easy, so the focus is on what is current and relatively insignificant, on everything that signifies all is going on as usual. When something happens which exposes the mutual pretense, both parties must pretend that nothing has happened. Here is where the ultimate in social tact is required, as in the incident referred to by the authors of a man who unexpectedly stumbled on a lady in his bathtub, and carefully closing the door murmured, "Pardon me, sir!" If a patient accidently refers to his dying, the nurse or doctor will pretend to misunderstand him. A nurse may take special pains not to walk in unexpectedly on a patient who is crying. Pretense must be added to the basic pretense because of all the slips that occur.

When a patient initiates this pretense, the staff can be quite relieved. So can the family. Embarrassment and other strains are reduced. A mood of "cautious serenity" may prevail. The rule of tact can create a sense of human dignity which is quite impressive. Patient, staff, and family all give credit to each other for performing well. A feeling of satisfaction—even the satisfaction of dying appropriately—can occur. If you have any doubts about these possibilities, read John Gunther's *Death Be Not Proud.*[8] The interaction between his adolescent son and the staff, relatives, and friends is most moving and very dignified. But other consequences are possible. Conditions occur which render maintenance of this context difficult. Increasing pain or rapid physical deterioration make the game difficult to play. Anxiety and panic may remove the false faces. The patient may become apathetic or oscillate between pretense and apathy. Moreover, although some terminal patients like the privacy they receive in this context, others feel isolated and cut off. As one woman said to her chaplain: "My family doesn't talk to me. It is as if I'm already dead. They won't even say good-by!" Yet I have seen good-bys exchanged without words in the midst of mutual pretense. Isolation is not at all inevitable in such a situation. It is rather difficult to gauge the extent to which the mutual-pretense context lends dignity or takes it away.

The fourth and final context to consider is "open awareness," when both patient and staff know that he is dying and both acknowledge the fact. It is clear that this context eliminates some of the problems created by the other three. Yet we should not minimize the problems involved. Glaser and Strauss point out that these are complex for two reasons.

The first relates to the matter of the time of death and the mode of dying. With respect to time there are two questions, of which one is: "*Am* I going to die?" This refers to the certainty of death. The other is: "*When* am I going to die?" Or the other question may be: "When will I know whether or not I am going to die?" Moreover, patient and staff are concerned about the mode of dying. Will there be severe pain that cannot be eliminated? Will there be loss of rationality? Will there be a coma, a prospect of living like a "vegetable" before finally dying? The importance of these questions is obvious. Thus the open awareness context involves inquiries such as: "Will I die?" "When will I die?" "How will I die?"

The basic point to make here is that *when there is open awareness of the certainty of death, it is not necessarily accompanied by open awareness as to the time of death and mode of dying.* There may be closed awareness of the time of death and suspicion awareness about the mode of dying. And the kinds of awareness can shift back and forth. For this reason, the open awareness context is complicated.

The second reason for complication concerns style of dying. Once you know that you are going to die, how are you going to go about it? How is the patient going to present his dying self to the world? His style will be judged by the patient himself, and it will be judged by everyone else who is involved with him. The list of what is considered appropriate behavior by the staff is endless. Some of the unwritten rules are: The patient should maintain relative composure and cheerfulness; he should face death with dignity; he should not cut himself off from the world; he should cooperate with the staff members who care for him; and certainly he should not shop around for impossible cures! If the patient's standards are identical with those of the staff and family, there is no problem. That is, no problem exists if he can live up to them. But there are vast cultural, social, and personal differences at large in any hospital. Some patients believe, for instance, that it is quite appropriate to commit suicide; to go home to die; to show violent feelings of grief; or no longer to put up with pills and needles. So open awareness tends to create a situation of conflict between the patient and the staff. The result is an attempt at education. The staff—especially the nurses—give signals as to what is unacceptable and acceptable. This may be done indirectly or rather directly—by commanding, scolding, coaxing, and calling on the doctor, chaplain, or others for reinforcement. In some cases the patient may try to educate the staff. The basic interaction is characterized as one of *negotiation*. A patient will agree to accept a certain routine if he can put off having his bath. A nurse will remove his uneaten food if the patient promises to quiet down and stop complaining. If a patient tries to negotiate too persistently and harshly, he may be relatively abandoned by the staff. "If you behave, I'll come and talk with you." And a dying patient sometimes negotiates, "Stay with me now and I'll be all right" (that is, I won't make a fuss).

Finally, it should be noted that in this setting there is the possibility for a patient to finish important work, plan his family's future, and make appropriate farewells. There is opportunity for reconciliation between man and man and between man and God. Open awareness can reduce strain on the family and produce a real satisfaction about the event of dying. But the contrary may occur. The patient may die with less dignity and more anguish than if he had been unaware of dying. The family and staff can become quite upset by his behavior. So again—as in the cases of closed awareness, suspicion awareness, and mutual pretense awareness—the problem is complex and the data confusing.

These awareness contexts can be useful tools, not only for members of the helping professions and the terminally ill, but also for you. There is a story about a man who signed a pact with the devil and gained as his reward the privilege of receiving the daily newspaper one day in advance. His purpose was foreknowledge of lottery results. The first time around he got the newspaper and discovered the winning number. But his elation quickly subsided for he accidently glimpsed the obituary page and saw his own name! Let us suppose that you have just signed a pact with an angel and could have foreknowledge of your own death.

1. If your physician knew that you had a terminal illness and would respond to you in any way you desired, what type of awareness context would you be *most likely* to set up?

Closed ———

Suspicion ———

Mutual pretense ———

Open ———

What type of awareness context would you *hope* to set up?

Closed ———

Suspicion ———

Mutual pretense ———

Open ———

2. Suppose that you could be told right now the exact time and exact mode of your death. The time revealed might be thirty years from now or five minutes. The mode could be natural causes, illness, homicide, or suicide; dying could be a long or short process, and painless or painful. Try to realize what is involved and then answer as accurately as you can. Would you want to know the truth on both items, on one of them, or neither?

Time of death: Yes ——— Mode of Death: Yes ———

No ———   No ———

Understanding these four types of awareness contexts should keep us from oversimplifying our reactions. It is not the case that the patient is simply aware or unaware of the fact that he is dying. It is not the case that the physician simply tells or does not tell the "truth." Any of the four awareness contexts may serve the patient positively, and any one of them can create problems for the patient. The situation of the terminally ill is complicated and confusing.

There is a growing movement in favor of open awareness and

against closed awareness. The thrust of this movement is as dangerous as that of the previous tradition. The term "denial" is used superficially, indiscriminately, and perhaps defensively as well. It becomes the enemy just as death is the enemy for the traditional doctor. Then one is unable to see the benefits of denial in another human being. We are all in the trap of seeing only what we need to see. The unexpected is either not seen at all, seen erroneously to confirm our expectations, or seen correctly, and we become quite anxious in this challenge to our understanding. This means that those who follow the cause of open awareness will not tend to see the benefits of denial at all, and when they are forced to see them, will explain them away. In my own experience, I have found that the "cheerful denyer" makes me anxious. I then project this anxiety onto the patient, seeking clues to all the anxiety that *must* be in him. Perhaps the patient is anxious, although quite unconscious of it. But why try to make him conscious of it? For his sake, or for mine?

Naturally I would not be considering the area of death and dying without some bias in favor of open awareness. If you are caught by this bias, then be careful. Indeed, be careful whatever your bias. Is awareness of death and dying useful? *Maybe* it is, sometimes, for some people. Maybe not—sometimes—for some people. What times and what people? There is no general answer. And there is little enough wisdom available to apply to concrete situations.

This exercise has been organized around three questions: Do we make too much or too little of death? Is awareness of our own death even possible? Is awareness of death useful? There are no definite answers. Perhaps this is because we have not yet learned how to ask the questions. Or it may be that the better the questions, the less likely the possibility of answers. In any case, it is wise to perceive ourselves as did the man who said: "If one of us dies, I'll go to Paris."

Many know the tale of the Bagdad merchant who sent his servant out to buy provisions. The servant came back pale with fear, saying, "Master, just now in the bazaar I was jostled by a man in the crowd. I turned about, and I saw Death. He stared at me and made a threatening gesture. Therefore lend me your horse and I will ride away and thus avoid my fate. I will ride to Samarra where Death cannot find me." The merchant lent him his horse, and the servant mounted it and rode off as fast as he could gallop. And then the merchant himself went down to the bazaar, and as he strolled around he too saw Death standing in the throng. He approached him and said, "Why did you make a threatening gesture to my servant when you saw him earlier this day?" But Death replied, "That was not a threatening gesture—merely a start of surprise. You see, I was astonished to find your servant in Bagdad, for tonight I have an appointment with him in Samarra."[9]

Fear of Death and Life

Those who face the prospect of death may react in many different ways. We may deny the possibility, perhaps as did the well-known minister in Washington, D.C., whose last words to his wife in final illness were, "I'll see you in the morning." We may accept it as a friendly form of sleep as did the poet Heine with the thought, "Death, it is the cool night." Or we may envision death as the great Destroyer, Atropos with her shears and Time with his scythe, who must be fought to the bitter end. This was the reaction of the Revolutionary War general Ethan Allen. When told by his parson, "General Allen, the angels are waiting for you," he replied, "Waiting are they? Well, God damn 'em, let 'em wait!"

But the most common reaction, and that which often underlies denial, acceptance, and defiance, is fear. Shakespeare has Claudio affirm:

> Ay, but to die, and go we know not where;
> To lie in cold obstruction, and to rot;
> This sensible warm motion to become
> A kneaded clod; and the delighted spirit
> To bathe in fiery floods, or to reside
> In thrilling regions of thick-ribbed ice;
> To be imprison'd in the viewless winds,
> And blown with restless violence round about
> The pendent world; or to be worse than worst

Of those that lawless and incertain thought
Imagine howling!—'tis too horrible!
The weariest and most loathed worldly life
That age, ache, penury, and imprisonment
Can lay on nature is a paradise
To what we fear of death.[1]

We are afraid. So the most popular scripture read at funerals contains the assurances, "Let not your hearts be troubled, neither let them be afraid," and "Yea, though I walk through the valley of the shadow of death, I shall fear no evil." (A wise wag added to the latter, "for I'm the meanest son-of-a-bitch in the valley.")

This exercise on our own fear of death is divided into three parts: universality of fear, fears of death, fears of life. The dynamics to be explored are suggested by the title of one of Alexander King's books, *Is There Any Life After Birth?*

Universality of Fear

Pronouncements abound that we will always fear our own death—or to the contrary, that we need not fear our own death. And rather convincing examples of both positions exist. On the one hand, according to Samuel Johnson, death is a terrible thing and to be feared. Boswell records:

JOHNSON. "No rational man can die without uneasy apprehension . . . I have made no approaches to a state whch can look on it as not terrible." BOSWELL. "In prospect death is dreadful; but in fact we find that people die easy." JOHNSON. "Why Sir, most people have not *thought* much of the matter, so cannot *say* much, and it is supposed they die easy. Few believe it certain they are then to die; and those who do, set themselves to behave with resolution, as a man does who is going to be hanged. He is not the less unwilling to be hanged." MISS STEWARD. "There is one mode of the fear of death, which is certainly absurd; and that is the dread of annihilation, which is only a pleasing sleep without a dream." JOHNSON. "It is neither pleasing, nor sleep; it is nothing. Now mere existence is so much better than nothing, that one would rather exist even in pain, than not exist. . . . The lady confounds annihilation, which is nothing, with the apprehension of it, which is dreadful. It is in the apprehension of it that the horror of annihilation consists."[2]

On the other hand, C. G. Jung's experience of a heart attack followed by visions during unconsciousness reveals little fear. He recalls:

It seemed to me that I was high up in space. Far below I saw the globe of the earth, bathed in a gloriously blue light. I saw the deep blue sea and the continents . . . I knew that I was on the point of departing from the earth . . . I had the feeling that everything was being sloughed away; everything I aimed at or wished for or thought, the whole phantasmagoria of earthly existence, fell away or was stripped from me— an extremely painful process. Nevertheless something remained; it was as if I now carried along with me everything I had ever experienced or done, everything that had happened around me. I might also say: it was with me, and I was it. I consisted of all that, and I felt with great certainty: this is what I am. "I am this bundle of what has been, and what has been accomplished." . . . I had everything that I was, and that was everything.[3]

For Johnson annihilation is horrible, whereas for Jung it is holy. A third example illustrates both the presence and absence of fear in one individual, Ivan Ilych. Tolstoy records with clinical accuracy:

. . . There was no deceiving himself: something terribly new and more important than anything before in his life, was taking place within him, of which he alone was aware. . . . Suddenly he felt the old, familiar, dull gnawing pain, stubborn and serious. There was the same familiar loathsome taste in his mouth. His heart sank and he felt dazed. . . . "Yes, life was there and now it is going, going and I cannot stop it." A chill came over him, his breathing ceased, and he felt only the throbbing of his heart.

"When I am not, what will there be? There will be nothing. Then,

where shall I be when I am no more? Can this be dying? No, I don't
want to!"

And suddenly it grew clear to him that what had been oppressing
him and would not leave him was all dropping away at once from two
sides, from ten sides, and from all sides. He was sorry for them, he must
act so as not to hurt them: release them and free himself from these
sufferings. "How good and how simple!" he thought. "And the pain?"
he asked himself. "What has become of it? Where are you, pain?"

He turned his attention to it.

"Yes, here it is. Well, what of it? Let the pain be."

"And death . . . where is it?"

He sought his former accustomed fear of death and did not find it.
"Where is it? What death?" There was no fear because there was no
death.

In the place of death there was light.

"So that's what it is!" he suddenly exclaimed aloud. "What joy!"⁴

These examples of attitudes toward death raise a host of issues. The circumstances of each were quite different. Johnson
was imagining his own death. Jung was in a critical state of
health, but not dying. And Ilych was clearly dying. Whether
death is eventually possible, quite likely in the immediate future, or a certainty in the immediate future may give rise to
different responses. And if the cause of eventual death is terminal illness, there is the possibility that responses will vary along
the path of dying as did those of Ilych.

There is room for considerable psychological speculation as
well. We have had long practice in the art of coping with anxiety, so our defenses rise quickly to master it. Repression of fear
in a terminal patient may lead to excessive normal activity and
resistance to therapeutic procedures. The fear may be handled
by supreme reliance on the magical, omnipotent figure of the
physician who appears to have come to the rescue. Relief of
pain may become the consuming desire, and successful relief
may be interpreted as release from the danger of death. Or the

fear may be displaced onto a minor ailment or minor aspect of the disease. A nurse who worked with the dying gently but firmly maintained that she had no fear of death. She did not appear at all frightened or defensive during discussion of our own fears. Afterwards she noted that although she was not afraid of death or dying, she was very anxious about the possibility of being buried alive. It seems reasonable to speculate that her fear of death was displaced onto a specific mode of dying (unlikely at that, and therefore safe).

The passage from Jung is awsome. For a more romantic example, listen to Walt Whitman:

> Come, lovely and soothing death,
> Undulate round the world, serenely arriving, arriving,
> In the day, in the night, to all, to each,
> Sooner or later, delicate death.[5]

We can be sentimental about Billy the Kid, Al Capone, Isolde, Juliet, and war. We can be sentimental about death per se. Romantic literature contains a "hearts and flowers" attitude about annihilation. Such euphoric responses can be little more than psychic flight from the reality of fear. Death may be a soothing, satisfactory companion to an elderly person who has had a "full" life, has outlasted family and friends, no longer feels worthwhile, is unable to function as accustomed, and is in great physical pain. But a young person's proclamation of death as a friend or lover is probably an act of desperation rather than joy. There may be something sentimental also about the individual who does not fear his own death, but only the consequences it might have on loved ones. Arnold Toynbee reflects:

I guess that if, one day, I am told by my doctor that I am going to die before my wife, I shall receive the news not only with equanimity but with relief. This relief, if I do feel it, will be involuntary. I shall be ashamed of myself for feeling it, and my relief will, no doubt, be tempered by concern and sorrow for my wife's future after I have been taken from her. At the same time, I do guess that, if I am informed that

I am going to die before her, a shameful sense of relief will be one element in my reaction. . . . This is, as I see it, the capital fact about the relation between living and dying. There are two parties to the suffering that death inflicts; and, in the apportionment of this suffering, the survivor takes the brunt.[6]

Such reflections are common among marriage partners. There is nobility in the thought that the survivor suffers more than the deceased. Of course it would be difficult to claim that this is always the case, especially when the prolonged suffering of a terminal cancer patient is considered. And there is reason to wonder how much this concern for the effects of one's own death on loved ones amounts to flight from fear of annihilation.

In such a discussion as this, it should be remembered that a negative emotion is not necessarily negative functionally. Fear is a signal of danger. As with physical pain, we would be in great difficulty without it. Fear is a sign of possibility as well as impossibility. As a contemplative exercise, consider the deaths of Socrates and Jesus. There appeared to be no fear in the former and great fear in the latter. Which death would you prefer? Why? An answer requires careful consideration. Even when fear of death is present, it may not be as dysfunctional as we are inclined to think.

Finally, beware of those who dwell on our supposed flight from fear. We who do fear death undoubtedly have a need to assure ourselves that others fear just as we do. From the trend of the above comments, I doubt that I am sufficiently open to the possibilities of not fearing death. In his statement, "My Own Death," one person wrote: "I am not afraid of death—I don't think about my own death. Maybe that's why I'm not afraid." He could be wrong about the reason. Another wrote:

I am hopeful that I will be able to consciously experience my own death, to savor its coming and complete take-over, till the final moment. . . . Perhaps my greatest fear is that I won't have this experience of death. Two times in my life I have had experiences when I thought

I would die, or when I thought that the experience I was undergoing was likened to dying. Both were good experiences; both, hopefully, will be experienced again in real death.

There is no reason to challenge automatically the positive attitude of this statement. No clinical study demonstrates that fear of death is universal. There is some clinical evidence to the contrary. In the midst of a serious operation from which she was not expected to recover, an elderly woman dreamed of walking through the grassy fields of paradise with her mother holding one hand and Jesus the other. On becoming conscious, she was furious with the doctors for having brought her back to life. It seems sensible to conclude that neither fear nor joy are universal responses to death.

Fears of Death

The fear of death is no simple response with simple causes. It has many components and is a different reaction for each one of us. It is shaped by such factors as age and state of physical health, family, social and religious backgrounds, and degree of psychological maturity. Events of the day may influence the degree of fear. As one individual perceived:

Death is threatening as hell sometimes—so much so that it seems as though one could not stand up to it. But at other times it seems less threatening. This seems to be related to how I feel about myself. It's been a good week. Life has been good to me the last several weeks. And today has been a very good day. Therefore, death somehow seems less threatening to me tonight. I can't guarantee the same will be true tomorrow or the next day.

Also, our conscious fears may be little more than self-deceptions which cover up more accurate reactions to death. But we must begin with ourselves where we can—with our conscious fears and an oversimplified analysis. We shall look at ourselves according to three categories: those of us who fear what happens after death occurs, those of us who fear the process of dying, and those of us who fear the loss of life.[7] Your task is to find out where you seem to fit. You may find yourselves focusing on one element which seems to describe your kind of fear adequately; or you may find nothing really appropriate and be forced to consider other possibilities. In any case, I offer only stimulus, and you must do the work.

The first category of fears includes those which relate to what happens *after death occurs.* I shall mention three kinds of fear in this category and you may desire to add others.

The first fear is about the fate of the body. The picture of a decaying, rotting body is not pleasant. So we try embalming, sturdy caskets, and even graves lined with metal. Some prefer cremation as an escape. Many of us refuse permission for autopsies and will not offer our bodies for medical education—even though we intellectually approve of such practices. Most people cannot picture their own bodies after they have died. We can visualize our funerals and the reactions of others to our death, but it is too much to actually imagine our own corpse. If you did not try this during the first exercise, try it now.

A second fear relating to what happens after death is fear of judgment. We know this has a long history, and it is understandable that anyone raised to believe in the possibility of final punishment is likely to be concerned about it. But we should not make the mistake of assuming that such fear does not occur in certain modern Protestants who believe only in the saccharine heaven of a nice-guy God. Nor is the contemporary agnostic or atheist necessarily free of the same fear. These long-standing and nearly universal beliefs in judgment would not have occurred without profound basis in our human experience, and the experience continues whether or not beliefs are clearly articulated.

The final fear in this category pertains to the unknown. Responding to their own death, people have written:

Death is something that I fear because I do not and feel that I cannot understand it. . . .

The unknown is my first thought with anxiety as an accompanying feeling. Death is a separation from all that is familiar. . . .

For some of us, death is seen as Hamlet saw it, as an "undiscovered country from whose bourn no traveler returns," and our response is at least uncertainty and often fear. It may be that this fear will increase in our generation as the charts of the afterlife so carefully detailed by traditional beliefs fade away.

Now we turn from fear of what happens after death to the category of fear related to the *process of dying*. Fear of the process is quite different from the fears just described. As one individual wrote:

In thinking about my own death, I have much greater problems with the idea of dying than on the idea of death itself. I have anxieties concerning a long day to day struggle to either live or die. I'm afraid it would feel cowardly not to fight for life in the face of a fatal illness and feel I would be constantly torn between wanting to "make a brave fight" and "giving up."

Some psychiatrists have observed this fear of the process of dying to be far more common than the fear of death itself or the afterlife. As before, I will mention three kinds of fear in this category, and you may desire to supply others.

The first is fear of pain. One individual put it simply: "Death = pain = fear." We tend to see dying as painful. It is the last "struggle." In the Christian tradition it was thought that evil forces would be contesting for the soul and that separation of the soul from the body was exceedingly painful. Nowadays, we often assume that dying is physically agonizing. Laymen tend to equate cancer and pain. And dying can be painful. Modern drugs are not always effective. To stop pain, some terminal patients request euthanasia or attempt suicide.

A second fear about the process of dying is the fear of indignity. Some of us are ashamed to participate in dying. We die in a hospital more frequently these days, and as patients we do not look our best. To be in a bed is embarrassing. A woman may not have her makeup on or her hair fixed just right. The room or the bedclothes may be untidy. There may be a bedpan or medical paraphernalia connected with the body—that is, there are certain intimate doings with the body which are not thought fit for the public eye. There may well be an odor which bothers the patient. More than this, disease may have ravaged both body and mind. The patient may show emotions, negative *and* positive, which are not customary. And the way some patients are treated by some poorly trained staff increases indignity. Not all deaths are dignified.

The final fear in this category is the fear of being a burden. There is no question about the fact that we are likely to be burdens. Few of us will die by accident, and modern medicine prolongs our dying. The dying patient in a hospital is a physical burden to those who visit him every day. He is a tremendous emotional burden, giving rise to all sorts of contradictory feelings among the family. He is the cause of strong feelings of sympathy, tenderness, and love, but also of disgust, pity, hate, and guilt. And of course in this day and age the patient is a financial burden. Seeing oneself as a possible burden is realistic.

Rather than fearing what happens after death or what happens during the process of dying, many of us fear death as the *loss of life*. Corliss Lamont writes:

To try to realize that when once we close our eyes in death, we shall never open them again on any happy or absorbing scene . . . to try to realize this, even to phrase such thoughts, can occasion a black, sinking spell along the pathways of sensation.[8]

Or, as another responded about his own death:

Cuts off—cuts off my reactions to "death," my reactions to "life," cuts off my reactions to people, and it cuts off me. A blind butcher. . . . To the Butcher: SHOVE IT.

As before, I shall mention three kinds of fear which give rise to such a spell and rage.

The first fear is of the loss of mastery. In this case, death represents the end of control over life. We all seek such mastery. We desire to control ourselves, to control others, and to control our life situations. We want to be active rather than passive, to participate in and change our present circumstances. But dying and death spell the end of our attempts to master.

I guess I fear dying because it involves a real loss of control. When you are dying, you have almost no control. There is an incredible vulnerability—and that's scary. It is almost as if one's last few minutes of life involve a vulnerability akin to one's first few minutes of life. Losing control over a body and environment which were at one time your servants must be a frightening experience.

The second fear of death as the loss of life is related to incompleteness and failure. The psychologist G. Stanley Hall concluded: "Fear of death is only the obverse of the love of life . . . We love life supremely and cannot have enough of it. . . . We want to live out completely all that is in us."[9] This is to say that we have ambitions. Men want to finish out their vocational life; women want to see their children raised and settled with a life of their own; youth want to at least get a good start going. One of the latter wrote: ". . . When I think of death for *me* I become angry because there are so many things I know I will not have finished, tasted, experienced and learned." We have goals to reach, but death does not respect them. We fear it because it destroys opportunity.

Finally, we fear death because it means separation. This is a most common and most complicated fear. We all express some sadness and many have a real dread of being taken away from those we love. Many have expressed their reaction to death in a way similar to the following:

When I think of my own death, I fear it because of the separation from my family and friends. I think there is a hereafter which somewhat reassures me because eventually I'll be reunited with those I know on earth.

Such fear is increased in our society by our reaction to the dying. We are so overwhelmed by the impending disaster and so afraid to speak of death to the dying that our relationships can be destructive. The dying often realize that we are abandoning them. It is no wonder that this specific fear is the most common of the nine fears described.

After this review of three categories and nine examples of fear, you should have some awareness of the focus of your own response to death. Which fear or fears, or what other fears, best describe your situation?

1. Which of the following categories pertains most to your way of fearing death? Check only *one* of the categories. This forces you to indicate the general focus of your fear.

> I do not fear death ___
> Fear of what happens after death ___
> Fear of the process of dying ___
> Fear of the loss of life ___
> Other (be brief, use only a word or two)
> _____

2. Which of the following ways of fearing death describe your reactions the most? *Check as many items as you wish.* This enables you to indicate the spread of your fears.

> (Fears of what happens after death)
> Fate of the body ___
> Judgment ___
> The unknown ___
> Other (be brief, use only a word or two)
> _____

(Fears of the process of dying)
    Pain   ____
    Indignity   ____
    Being a burden   ____
    Other (be brief, use only a word or two)

(Fears of the loss of life)
    Loss of mastery   ____
    Incompleteness   ____
    Separation   ____
    Other (be brief, use only a word or two)

---

3. What degree of difficulty do you have in looking at your
   own fears of death?
                No difficulty   ____
                Little difficulty   ____
                Fair amount of difficulty ____
                Much difficulty   ____
                Great difficulty   ____

While reflecting on your responses, consider what surprises
you about them and about the process of acknowledgment. If
you have opportunity to discuss your responses with others, you
will probably discover that fears of the loss of life are more
common than fears of the process of dying, and that the latter
fears are more common than fears of what happens after death.
Somewhat ominous exceptions are members of the health professions, who tend to focus on the process of dying. Fear of the unknown and fear of separation are the leading reactions in the other
categories. Of course you will discover that the extent of fear and
degree of difficulty in looking at one's own fear vary greatly.

Fears of Life

Now we turn to an implication of the fears we have just
labeled for ourselves. It is an idea you are familiar with but it

deserves attention nevertheless. As Alexander King put it: "Is there any life after birth?"

It has been argued that death could not be a problem for man. If we are alive, then death does not yet exist and we have no reason to be concerned about it. When we are dead, then we no longer exist and are unable to be concerned. So death is no problem. I used to believe that this argument was nothing but superficial sophistry and totally inadequate to explain away our many strong fears of death. But perhaps the reasoning is right, at least to the extent that the fear of death is secondary and not our basic fear. Death is an ultimate mystery. Such a mystery makes an excellent screen on which to project all our concerns about life. The fear of death is a projection of our most basic fear. *Our fear of death is really our fear of life.* All the fears so far described may function as appropriate responses to the facts of our lives, and it is in life that we have learned them. Fear is a useful response to many aspects of reality. But it can be irrational, a symptom of our inability to cope creatively with the experience of living. This irrational fear may rule our responses to death.

Consider the category of what happens after death and fear about the fate of the body. This fear is understandable. According to biblical tradition and modern psychosomatic medicine, *we are our bodies.* We cannot separate our body from our self. A man who loses an arm or a woman who has a breast removed faces a different body and goes through a period of developing a new self as well. So fear about the fate of the body is to be expected. But some of us are caught by this fear more than any other. This may happen when our living is focused on the body. Farmers, unskilled laborers, and professional models would be prone to this fear. So also would those whose bodies have been made defective through heredity, accident, or disease. But there is another group which is not quite so natural. Hypochondriacs tend to be somewhat withdrawn from the world and highly concerned about their physical sensations. Those who fear the fate of the body may be the same, retreating from most of the aspects of life to emphasize this one aspect of the self. For the self is not only body, it is comprised of other elements, especially other people. Those who fear dissolution of the body may be those who have discarded the world and become preoccupied with a narrow view of themselves. This kind of fear of what happens after death is understandable, but it may reveal a narrow and fearful view of life.

Judgment is an inherent aspect of human life. We do commit serious wrongs and when we do not feel we have atoned or been forgiven, we anticipate a final reckoning. In addition, we all have a tendency to elevate our guilt and make the most of it. Little errors become offenses against the whole of life and against God. Life treats us harshly, but this is appropriate because we are so guilty. And of course life after death must be eternal punishment. It should be noted that this stance contains a great deal of pride. It is no small thing to be beyond forgiveness. For those who cannot find and accept compassion, death is the bitter end, and for some an even more bitter beginning. The fear of judgment after death is understandable, but it can reveal our extreme guilt in the midst of life.

It is perfectly natural to wonder about the unknown, and perhaps even to have some trepidation about any great and permanent change. But to really fear what comes next is something else. Those who are afraid of what comes after death because it is unknown may tend to be those who cannot face the unknown in life. Many of us lack the spirit of adventure. Any novelty or surprise comes as a shock which immobilizes. Our daily lives are dedicated to the goal of minimizing risk and fostering routine. We may not like the life we lead, but all possibilities for something different are refused for the sake of protecting what little satisfaction we have. New opportunity is equated with chaos. The old things must be done just right without any error or variation. Such a person runs scared and backward through life. Moreover, since some risks must be taken in the world, we encourage others to do this for us. It may be our parents, spouse, children, or friends who face life and take our risks. Unfortunately, no one can take the risk of death for us. So if we find our fear of death focused on the unknown, it may be that our way of life in this world is cowardly.

Turning to the category of the process of dying, we note that fear of pain can be realistic. But quite a few doctors and patients who have been close to death assert that dying is not usually so painful as we tend to believe.

Why are some of us so afraid of the pain of dying? We learn it in part from each other. The endless gossip of mankind is apt to dwell repeatedly and with relish on the alarming side of things—even seek it out and enlarge it. We get into the habit of expecting dreadful pain. Moreover, if a small injury or illness can be painful, there is a certain logic in imagining that the ultimate physical failure must be the ultimate in pain. This is not at all necessarily true.

But perception of pain also depends on matters other than physical. An American adult male will faint at the supposed pain of a hypodermic needle while a child of another culture will ask for the needle the way he asks a GI for a chocolate. So the pain of an illness from which you know you are going to die is quite likely to be greater than the pain of an illness from which you know you are going to recover. But even granting knowledge of death, awareness of pain will be different in people. Emotional suffering can increase physical suffering. Experience of pain may well be more acute in a patient who feels abandoned. Those who suffer only for themselves may feel great pain, while those who see their suffering in the broader context of other people may suffer less. On the whole, those who fear pain the most and will suffer it the most may be those who have difficulties in human relationships and are preoccupied with themselves. If we fear the pain of dying, it is possible that we have found no meaningful cause outside of ourselves which makes pain—the pain of dying and the pain of living—endurable and even acceptable.

The fear of indignity can also be carried beyond reason. There are those who have been raised to believe that all sickness should be concealed. It is interpreted as personal weakness, as almost immoral. They go through life putting up a good front only to be exposed at the end and consumed by embarrassment or guilt. There are others whose fear of indignity in dying may reveal a whole life orientated around avoidance of shame. Their basic concern is the social opinion of others. They are not withdrawn from society, but only superficially connected. They live in order to win social approval, and they fear the slightest *faux pas*. Their most terrible nightmares are commonly dreams of appearing in public without their pants or entirely naked. But to die is to drop your pants. For those of us who have this superficial relationship with society, fear of the indignity of dying may be extreme.

Consider the fear of being a burden. Such a fear can be realistic, but perhaps those ruled by this dread are those who cannot accept gifts gracefully. Some of us cannot tolerate being helped by others. Either we avoid help, or we pay for it in advance, or we pay the helper back as soon as possible. Now, some of us are too dependent on others, but the opposite extreme is no more sensible. We are all interdependent. To some people we are eternally in debt and there is no way out of it. Regardless of what we think of our parents, for example, we would not be as mature and emotionally sound as we are if they had not contributed far more than we are commonly inclined to acknowledge. Attempting to maintain a life and death of independence is absurd. We should note that the source of this absurdity is in fact probably a strong feeling of dependence. The seemingly too-independent person is usually fighting against more basic dependency needs. Those who are like this, who feel threatened by help from others, will likely fear the burdensome process of dying.

The first fear in the category of loss of life is that of loss of mastery. There are at least two types of people who accentuate this fear. Some people are overconcerned about self-control. Many of these are afraid of losing consciousness; they fear taking drugs and fight against falling asleep. In becoming unconscious, one does lose self-control. Others are plagued by the fear that they may go insane at some time in the future. Insanity is the loss of self-control. Those of us who have such abnormal needs to master ourselves may see death as the ultimate defeat. Then there are people who are overconcerned about control of others. Any of us who are highly aggressive and domineering in our families or our vocations do not want our power diminished or destroyed. What we do in life is done in part subtly for the sake of maintaining and increasing our rule. Those of us who have this need to master others will also tend to see death as the great defeat. Perhaps such needs are reflected in the admittedly worthy causes of preplanning funerals and euthanasia. Whether with respect to ourselves or to others, some of us have an overwhelming desire to play God. Indeed, we all have this problem to some degree. Death is feared because it destroys our illusions of grandeur.

The fear of death as incompleteness and failure may occur in those people who never finish anything, who fail at whatever they attempt. And there are some who see themselves as failures in life even though this is not the case. There is a report about a middle-aged woman who was married to and ruled by an extremely perfectionistic man. She was dying of cancer, became depressed, and eventually revealed that she thought her life to be a failure. Seeing herself only through the eyes of her husband, she could not appreciate her own accomplishments. Some of us are perfectionistic about ourselves. Everyone has had big dreams about his future. But life whittles these down to size. If we are mature, we acknowledge and accept our limitations and those of our situation. If we cannot do so, we tend to see ourselves as failures. Death is then feared as a forced retirement, and we will fight for one more chance to make up or add another achievement. In our obsessively productive society, retirement is death and death is retirement. Death equals unemployment.

The very last fear in the category of loss of life is separation. Because this fear strikes us as so very realistic, we are inclined to skirt discussion of its frequent relation to corrupt varieties of love. Some men die with fear of leaving their mothers expressed in their last words. Currently, we are not so impressed by such extreme expressions of filial piety. The fear of leaving one's mother suggests a corrupt and even incestuous relationship. Some women at the point of death fear separation from their children. But they may be ruthless tyrants who have dominated them. And fear of separation from one's spouse may occur because we are neurotically dependent and cannot stand to "go it alone" into death. Some grief over forthcoming separation arises out of anger and guilt toward the spouse. Any version of corrupt marital relations can serve to increase our fear of death as separation from our partially "loved ones." Psychologists have clinically observed that overly prolonged grief in the bereaved usually signifies a poor relationship with the one who died. The same conclusion applies to one who overintensely dreads death as separation. Thus any of us who are possessed by this particular fear may be expressing our problems with those we love.

The conclusion is that our fear of death is basically our fear of life. If our fears were rational they would not prevent us from looking at the inevitability of our own deaths and learning about ourselves and our lives. Since our fears are for the most part irrational, we run away from death, and what we are fleeing as well is our own life. And life is other people. What I am suggesting is that those who are withdrawn from others, who are consumed with guilt, who are too dependent, or independent, who are too ambitious or masterful, or too ashamed or proud—these are the ones who most fear death. We fear it because of the quality of our involvements with others. We are not all mentally ill by social definition, but we do have problems in living, especially in living with others. Our own death is a problem because our own daily living is a problem.

To conclude this exercise on our fears of death, the same point needs to be put positively. If it is the case that those of us who flee life will also flee death, then it may also be the case that *those of us who fully welcome life will welcome death as well.* This is not a philosophical speculation or theological proclamation. Fear of death does not exist when a person lives at the peak of happiness. At a moment of high joy, death is neither feared nor ignored, and it is often embraced. The poet Hölderlin truly affirmed: "Once I lived like the gods, and more is not needed." This insight is quite opposed to our usual thoughts about life and death. We tend to say: "I like life so much that I don't want to die." This may be an error, a rather important one. It is we who do *not* enjoy life enough who do not want to die. To put the matter crudely—and paradoxically: If you can't leave it, you don't like it; if you like it, you can leave it.

So if we can contemplate to possibility of our own death, we might ask ourselves: under what conditions would I be able to accept my having to die as a joyful conclusion to the experience of life? This is the kind of question a contemplative would take a lifetime to answer. Ten minutes is a more reasonable amount of time for others. Consider it carefully and then write a succinct answer. Your response will provide an orientation for dying, but more than this, it will offer an orientation for living.

There is one more question. To what extent does this analysis amount to a denial of death? What are we to make of all this psychologizing to the effect that fear of death is related to perception of oneself as inadequate and unloved? Our fears about living do lead to irrational fears of death. But stress on our irrational fear of death may serve as a way of minimizing our raitonal fear of it. Shakespeare introduces the passage on Claudio's fear as follows:

ISABELLA: What says my brother?
CLAUDIO: Death is a fearful thing.
ISABELLA: And shamed life a hateful.
CLAUDIO: Ay, but to die, and. . . .

"Ay, but to die——" It is not enough to focus only on the "shamed life" in itself and in relation to death. We need to remind ourselves that psychological understanding and sentiment can go hand in hand very nicely indeed. Seriously consider the possibility of death as a joyful conclusion to the experience of life, but do not forget the magic by which we deceive ourselves. This danger is put quite clearly in a short parable by John Fowles. He calls it, "The Prince and the Magician."

Once upon a time there was a young prince who believed in all things but three. He did not believe in princesses, he did not believe in islands, he did not believe in God. His father, the king, told him that such things did not exist. As there were no princesses or islands in his father's domains, and no sign of God, the young prince believed his father.

But then, one day, the prince ran away from his palace. He came to the next land. There, to his astonishment, from every coast he saw islands, and on these islands, strange and troubling creatures whom he dared not name. As he was searching for a boat, a man in full evening dress approached him along the shore.

"Are those real islands?" asked the young prince.

"Of course they are real islands," said the man in evening dress.

"And those strange and troubling creatures?"

"They are all genuine and authentic princesses."

"Then God must exist!" cried the prince.

"I am God," replied the man in full evening dress, with a bow.

The young prince returned home as quickly as he could.

"So you are back," said the father, the king.

"I have seen islands, I have seen princesses, I have seen God," said the prince reproachfully.

The king was unmoved.

"Neither real islands, nor real princesses, nor a real God exist."

"I saw them!"

"Tell me how God was dressed."

"God was in full evening dress."

"Were the sleeves of his coat rolled back?"

The prince remembered that they had been. The king smiled.

"That is the uniform of a magician. You have been deceived."

At this, the prince returned to the next land, and went to the same shore, where once again he came upon the man in full evening dress.

"My father the king has told me who you are," said the young prince indignantly. "You deceived me last time, but not again. Now I know that those are not real islands and real princesses, because you are a magician."

The man on the shore smiled.

"It is you who are deceived, my boy. In your father's kingdom there are many islands and many princesses. But you are under your father's spell, so you cannot see them."

The prince pensively returned home. When he saw his father, he looked him in the eyes.

"Father, is it true that you are not a real king, but only a magician?"

The king smiled, and rolled back his sleeves.

"Yes, my son, I am only a magician."

"Then the man on the shore was God."

"The man on the shore was another magician."

"I must know the real truth, the truth beyond magic."

"There is no truth beyond magic," said the king.

The prince was full of sadness.

He said, "I will kill myself."

The king by magic caused death to appear. Death stood in the door and beckoned to the prince. The prince shuddered. He remembered the beautiful but unreal islands and the unreal but beautiful princesses.

"Very well." he said. "I can bear it."

"You see, my son," said the king, "you too now begin to be a magician."[10]

GESTATION

Death in Life

Five centuries ago the plague known as the Black Death killed a quarter of the population of Europe within a period of three years. It was the worst disaster we know of that had befallen mankind. One response was flight. Those who could leave the towns did so. Those who could not and had authority, segregated themselves. But such a scourge cannot be fled successfully. The leading response became preoccupation with death. The art of the times reflects this. There was an interest in graves and corpses. Painters dwelt in detail on the sufferings of Christ, the terrors of the Last Judgment and the punishments of hell. Most popular were depictions of the Dance of Death. Many lived as Michelangelo wrote: "No thought is born in me that has not 'Death' engraved upon it."[1] The Black Death created a cultural "ego-chill," and the inevitable response was preoccupation with death.

Our preoccupation with it in the middle of the twentieth century is a response to a human rather than a biological plague. Urban blight, racial tension, conflict between the generations, wars, and the threat of nuclear holocaust are factors which have created an age of death. There is a sense of having come to an end—a dead end. We cannot flee, so we become preoccupied. Saul Bellow reflects:

But what is the philosophy of ths generation? Not God is dead, that period was passed long ago. Perhaps it should be stated death is God.

This generation thinks—and this is its thought of thoughts—that nothing faithful, vulnerable, fragile, can be durable or have any true power. Death waits for these things as a cement floor waits for a dropping light bulb.[2]

Death has become our companion. And some of us offer it a desperate welcome.

Just as our society has built its "ship of death," so also have individuals. Whatever man fears may also be desired. Human beings can and do choose to die. Albert Camus proclaimed:

There is but one truly serious philosophical problem and that is suicide. Judging whether life is or is not worth living amounts to answering the fundamental question of philosophy. All the rest . . . comes afterwards. These are games; one must first answer.[3]

Those who commit suicide have raised this question to some degree and acted upon a negative answer. And there are others, the living dead, who reach the same conclusion but do not bother to remove themselves from this life. For such people death is God, a companion who offers not less but more than life.

In this exercise we complete our descent. To focus on our own death is to perceive our denial. To perceive our denial is to face our fear of death. And to face our fear of death is to acknowledge our fear of life. Inevitably we are led to examine our own worship of death. Suicide is the subject. It is one which tends to expose or create more anxiety than others related to death. It gives rise to feelings, thoughts, and fantasies we would prefer to remain unaware of. And we response to the issues with defensive legalisms. This common reaction to the topic and to those who attempt and commit suicide is a clue that Camus is making a useful statement.

Yet exploration of suicide is not only a descent. The theme of this exercise is that the suicidally inclined do more than illustrate the basic question concerning life; they provide an answer which contains a truth to be acted upon. Proper participation in suicide, we will find presently, is death followed by gestation. We shall examine the possibility of our own suicide by approaching the issue along three lines: the prevalence of suicide, suicide as a problem, and prevention by permission.

Prevalence of Suicide

To look carefully at the prevalence of suicide is to discover its magnitude. According to the statistics, every day, every hour, almost every minute, somewhere in the world a human being is taking his life. In our nation it happens about 60 times a day, every day: 22,000 times a year. During the past twenty-four minutes, an American has destroyed himself. Suicide is tenth on the scale of top killers in the USA.

But these statistics are grossly inaccurate. County coroners or medical examiners who certify the nature of individual deaths often make mistakes and label a suicidal death as accidental. One coroner noted only a dozen suicidal deaths annually for a city of over half a million. It was discovered that he refused to consider any death as suicidal unless a suicide note was found! In one California county careful examination revealed the rate to be eight times higher than the statistics recorded. And the fact of suicide is frequently hidden due to pressure from survivors, clergy, and others.

So suicide is prevalent—more prevalent than we realize, and no one knows exactly how frequent. Its extent becomes even more apparent when we consider a typology of the act. Going beyond consideration of the means employed to the circumstances and attitude of the individual, we can distinguish between *direct* and *indirect* suicide. Direct suicide refers to those cases in which individuals play a conscious, intentional role in causing their own death. They do not just wait for death to occur, but actually cause it to take place. There are three common variations on this theme. First, there are those who openly *seek* their death by whatever means. The act is committed in such a manner that rescue is impossible or most unlikely. The second variation includes all those who already face the prospect of death in the near future and would like to hasten it along. They do not want to just let it happen but desire to play an active role. Because of the protracted delays made possible by modern terminal facilities, we hear of the older person in the last stages of a fatal illness who gathers remarkable strength, takes tubes out of himself, climbs out of bed, lifts a heavy window, and throws himself to the ground below. Ernest Hemingway's death may have been an example of this.

The third form of direct suicide is more subtle. It consists of those who consciously gamble with death. A classic example is one who plays "Russian roulette"—who holds a revolver to his temple with only one of the six chambers loaded (or with only one *un*loaded), and pulls the trigger. Of course the risks taken may be more obscure. Consider teen-agers, expert drivers, who play the game of "chicken." Two drivers aim their cars for collision or for a cliff, drive ahead at high speed, and the first one to swerve loses. This game may be a conscious flirting with death as well as a crude proclamation of manliness. Included in this variation are all those who attempt suicide in such a way that rescue *may* take place. The resulting death is part accident —the gambler has lost. The gambling element in direct suicide leads us to acknowledge that self-destruction may be far more prevalent than we realize.

But dealing only with the direct and willful taking of one's life is still superficial. Suicide also occurs indirectly. The motivation may be unconscious and subintentional. Nearly all these forms of self-destruction occur in ways which are entirely ignored by statistical studies. Some people go to hospitals in order to die, even though their illness is not terminal. These patients do die when there is no physiological reason for it. There are others with terminal illness who unconsciously hasten their death and die unexpectedly early. And there are patients without terminal illness who consistently *mismanage* their lives—the diabetic who does not keep to his diet or forgets to take his insulin, the man with a liver disease who continues heavy drinking, and the heart patient who refuses to follow a physician's orders about physical activity. Similar to such patients are people who have repeated accidents. The carelessness of both certain pedestrians and certain drivers is unconsciously calculated. Many of the "hard-luck champions" we know or have heard of are subintentionally seeking self-destruction. There are also those who provoke other people to murder. Some persons do not kill themselves, but get others to do it for them. As the reader will realize, this is a type of dynamic found commonly in marriages and in many cases of antisocial behavior. Crime does pay, if the real goal is to be caught, punished, and killed. One murderer on record refused all offers of pardon by his state governor and so was put to death by the state.

This list of varieties of indirect suicide would remain all too limited without mention of one other variation with far-reaching social consequences. Love of war at any cost is a dynamic frequently attributed to key political and military figures. The slogan "Better dead than Red" may be a result of projecting suicidal intentions onto the social scene. The identical dynamic may lie underneath the feeling that we are better off dead than members of the Establishment. Even the cry for peace, however valid on the surface, may reflect in some of us a cry for death. Imagine for a moment a most important room hidden somewhere in the bowels of this nation, which contains a row of ten buttons. Seven of these must be pushed to release the thermonuclear bombs which will destroy half the globe. An individual sits before each button. Five are "hawks" and five are "doves." The international crises mount until finally the head of the nation gives the signal to fire. Can it be reasonably assumed that there will be a stalemate with only the five "hawks" pressing their buttons? Hardly. It is quite possible that some of the "doves" would be among the first to release total destruction.

The philosopher Pascal once described a situation familiar to us all. We are invited to walk over a narrow wooden bridge, without railings, which stretches across a meadow. Of course we do not refuse the invitation. But when the same bridge spans a deep chasm, we are not so ready to accept the challenge. For here we discover the possibility, not just of making a mistake in footing, but of making an intentional error: committing suicide. And the more we fear walking over such a bridge, the more probable it is that we are encountering a powerfully repressed desire. The room with the buttons is such a bridge.

What is commonly suspected of those who devote themselves to the elimination of hard-core pornography might well be suspected of some of us who are devoted to the elimination of war. As there may be a desire to delight in pornography, so there may be a desire for total catastrophe. The desire for peace, however valid for the world and even genuine in the individual, may also mask and defend against the desire for destruction. This desire may have many motivations. One in particular is relevant at this point. Chronic anxiety is a state more undesirable than any other, and we will try almost any maneuver to eliminate it. Modern man is living in anxious anticipation of destruction. Such anxiety can be easily eliminated by self-destruction. As a German saying puts it: "Better an end with terror than a terror without end." So it is naïve to assume that our growing awareness of the possibility of nuclear holocaust will move our culture in the direction of peace in life. It may move us toward peace in death. Franklin D. Roosevelt's statement that we have nothing to fear but fear itself makes this point. Flight from anxiety can lead to irrational denial *or* irrational acceptance *or* irrational promotion of death.

Examination of statistical reports and of the varieties of direct and indirect suicide demonstrates that suicide is widespread. If you share your answers to the following questions with others, you will most probably discover this to be true even in your own immediate social situation.

1. Has either a close friend or member of your family *committed* suicide?   Yes____ No____
2. Has either a close friend or member of your family *attempted* suicide?   Yes____ No____
3. How often have you seriously considered committing suicide?

    Very often   ____
    Now and then   ____
    Seldom   ____
    Never   ____

4. Have you attempted suicide?

    Yes, with *high* probability of death   ____
    Yes, with *low* probability of death   ____
    No   ____

5. Have you participated in any form of indirect suicide?

    Yes   ____
    No   ____
    Uncertain   ____

Thus far the discussion has attempted to broaden our understanding of suicide without deviating from accepted understanding of the term. But there is another segment of mankind that finds death a suitable companion. When man is seen from the very pit of despair, it may be said that there are only three kinds of people: those who commit suicide, those who attempt it and fail, and those who do not even try. The later are the living dead. They may be the most common companions of death. And perhaps they are among us; perhaps they are ourselves.

The term "living dead" is not one we can define precisely. From the exterior, they may appear as one individual describes them:

[My] image corresponds to Shaw's feeling that "most people die at thirty and are buried at sixty." I look at the eyes of people—like on the subway—and at a stare as blank as that of a Greek statue, and say to myself, "They're dead already."

Far more useful is the description of the interior. The mood is indicated by the following statement:

When it's all over and I can no longer hide from the end of me, the absurdity will also be tragic and inescapable. To know that my *purpose* was not a mystery to be unearthed, but only a temporary puzzle to busy my imagination. To know that I will end is bad enough—at least I am still able to despair.

A third statement indicates the social death involved in such despair:

Death still presents me with the problem of how I experience things in my world. . . . When my senses are assaulted, and I close some of them down to escape into some silence or darkness, I notice the difference and the diminution of energy inside me. When I close off communication with other people, I feel the same kind of diminution afterward. So I guess I'm dying sometimes, but not finally because I always have to open up again. Death will be when I can't find the energy to re-establish contact, and while it is happening, I expect to feel increasingly more alone.

Eyes that stare blankly; being able only to despair; total loss of contact—these are symptoms of the living dead. Why do they not kill themselves? Some may be unaware that they are not alive. They have forgotten what it was like to be connected with life. Others may fear the process of postmortem dying. As Dorothy Parker understood it in her "Resume":

> Razors pain you;
> Rivers are damp;
> Acids stain you;
> And drugs cause cramp.

Guns aren't lawful;
Nooses give;
Gas smells awful;
Your might as well live.[4]

The most profound possibility is that even death offers no hope of release from despair. Those who attempt or commit suicide place their trust in death. The despairing who do not, can find no companion whatsoever. This is the "sickness unto death" which Kierkegaard fully understood. It is a sickness in which man is mortally ill but cannot die. This is the final impotence realized in despair. The despair of the living dead "is the disconsolateness of not being able to die."[5] For them, suicide is hardly the worst possible fate for man. That is reserved for those who are unable to commit it.

Camus, who was an expert perceiver of living death, tells this tale of a woman who died young, was buried late, and worshipped death in between.

She was a lonely and peculiar woman. She kept in close touch with the Spirits, took up their causes, and refused to see certain members of her family who had a bad reputation in this world where she found refuge.

One day, she received a small legacy from her sister. These five thousand francs, coming at the end of her life, turned out to be something of an encumbrance. They had to be invested. If almost everyone is capable of using a large fortune, the difficulty begins when the sum is a small one. The woman remained true to herself. Nearing death, she wanted shelter for her old bones. A real opportunity occurred. A lease had just expired in the local cemetery. On this plot the owners had erected a magnificent, soberly designed black marble tomb, a genuine treasure in fact, which they were prepared to let her have for four thousand francs. She purchased the vault. It was safe investment, immune to political upheavals or fluctuations in the stock market. She had the inner grave prepared and kept it in readiness to receive her body. And when everything was finished, she had her name carved on it in gold letters.

The transaction satisfied her so completely that she was seized with a veritable love for her tomb. At first, she went to see how the work was progressing. She ended up by paying herself a visit every Sunday afternoon. It was the only time she went out, and it was her only amusement. Toward two in the afternoon, she made the long trip that brought her to the city gates where the cemetery was. She would go into the little tomb, carefully close the door behind her, and kneel on the *prie-dieu*. It was thus, quite alone with herself, confronting what she was and what she would become, rediscovering the link in a chain still broken, that she effortlessly pierced the secret designs of Providence. A strange symbol even made her realize one day that in the eyes of the world she was dead. On All Saints' Day, arriving later than usual, she found the doorstep of her tomb piously strewn with violets. Some unknown and tenderhearted passers-by, seeing the tomb devoid of flowers, had had the kind thought of sharing their own, and honored her neglected memory.

. . . She was going to die, and her daughter dressed her for the tomb while she was alive. Actually, it seems it's easier to do so before the limbs are stiff. Yet it's odd all the same to live among people who are in such a hurry.[6]

This woman lived among the dead and was dead. We do not all demonstrate our living death so clearly. Few of us are so totally dead. Yet there are areas of living in which we are not alive. What are they? Take time now to consider areas of your present life in which you participate to some degree in living death. Does it occur in the area of family, friends, community, vocation, or some other realm? What was once alive in you and has been lost? What should have come alive and was stillborn? In what areas would you be believed to be dead—incapable of life—by those who know you intimately? Each one of us is reflected in the expressionless faces of the living dead.

How prevalent is suicide? In some sense, to some degree, it is nearly universal. Few of us will commit any form of direct suicide. But indirect suicide is another matter, and "living death" still another. Perhaps we are all already on the path, losing our lives and it is only a matter of time. Rilke prayed: "O

Lord, give each man his own death." The plea is unnecessary. An individual's death is almost inevitably his own. It is ironic that discussions of death often demonstrate our concern about children cut off before their time and middle-aged people cut off in their so-called "prime." The concern is legitimate, but requires more depth and breadth. For death rarely seeks out people; we seek out death.

And when we arrive, Death rightly proclaims: "You made your deathbed, now die in it!"

Suicide as a Problem

The attitude of our culture on the matter of suicide is quite clear: we do not like it and we want to stop it. Suicide is defined as a problem to be prevented. Our difficulty is determination of the nature of the problem. However common, suicide appears to us as a mysterious event. In an essay entitled, "Suicide as a Magical Act," Charles William Wahl defines it as such—"actuated to achieve irrational, delusional, and illusory ends."[7] His analysis is useful and illuminating. It is also misleading by its stress on the "magical" aspect of self-destruction.

We tend to think about suicide from the perspective of vast generalizations, concluding that human beings struggle to survive. Freud postulated that there are two basic instincts—a death instinct and a life instinct. His followers have dismissed the former and kept the latter. Neither seems to me a useful hypothesis. The concepts of life and death are gigantic abstractions. It is not likely that organisms are ruled by such generalities. Freud proposed that the unconscious has no awareness of death. He should have added the observation that it has no awareness of life either. Human beings are driven by a number of quite concrete needs. It is these concrete concerns that rule us and not the so-called need for life or for death. These concrete needs may be met by a variety of situations, and it follows that the events we call life and death may fulfill or not fulfill those specific needs. A need for giving and receiving love in a dying patient, for example, may be met by prolongation of life or by choosing or hastening death. It is not very useful, therefore, to assume a life instinct or even a will to survive in man.

Certainly suicide is often a magical act. But this is a misleading observation unless immediately followed by the statement that self-preservation is often an act based on equally illusionary goals. There are times when we wish to live and times when we wish to die. There is a wish for a full and meaningful life and a wish for a full and meaningful death. These wishes are probably magical in most of us, most of the time. In short: we are magicians. When we hear that suicide is irrational and magical, let us keep a useful perspective by remembering that the act of maintaining ourselves is usually no different. The awe that possesses us when we face suicide should possess us when we face ourselves at any time. (Of course the results of the magical act of suicide are irrevocable, and so appear more extreme than the magical act of living. Yet how many of us ever recover from the deeply laid magical patterns we have created? The distinction from this point of view is not so clear as we might like it to be.)

To become specific on the motivations behind suicide, we might explore a list such as that given by Herbert Hendin in *Suicide and Scandinavia:* death as retaliatory abandonment, as omnipotent mastery, as self-punishment, as a reunion, as a phenomenon that in an emotional sense has already taken place, as retroflexed murder, and as rebirth.[8] These are some, but not all, of the possible motivations. The following discussion will focus on only one aspect of suicide, which appears in many of the motivations just listed. Our culture concludes that suicide is basically an attack. The question to consider is: an attack on what?[9]

According to society, suicide is an attack on society. Until 1961, in England it was considered a felony, an act of murder.

Western law has found all sorts of reasons for justifiably killing others, but no reason for killing oneself. One who commits suicide must forfeit his property and good name. One who attempts it and fails may be punished for a criminal act. In this country this is still the case in a few states today. One hundred and fifty years ago, Blackstone stated the reason succinctly in his *Commentaries:* suicide is among the highest of crimes *because it is against the king.* Suicide is rude. An individual has a contract with society in the interest of general stability. Suicide breaks that contract, which in turn disintegrates the social structure. It is a clear enemy of society. Therefore, the bodies of suicides must be buried at the crossroads with stakes in their hearts—or at best, the suicidally inclined must be discovered and helped by suicide prevention centers.

But what really bothers a society about suicide? It is not just a matter of extreme autonomy and breaking of a social contract. Three things are involved. First, the suicide casts off the values prized by society and thereby causes it to question itself, recognize its limitations, and confess its pride. The suicide passes a judgment. Society does not care to examine the judgment, but in defense of itself as it is, condemns the suicide. So the understanding that the suicide is not closely involved with society is true, but whether this is to be automatically condemned is questionable. All judgment requires detachment. Second, we should ponder over the fact that this attack uses death as a weapon in a death-denying culture. The suicide breaks through our defenses against death, reminding us that we ourselves are fated to die and that we have the ability and perhaps even the desire to kill ourselves. An adolescent who commits suicide disturbs our glorification of youth. To place a positive value on death is too much for this or any other death-denying culture. Finally, it should be noted that the suicide frequently has the gall to suggest that a new society is available to replace the old one. This is the crowning blow. Whether it be with the saints and angels in heaven or with loved ones in the afterlife, many suicides exhibit a hope for something better. They die, not only out of despair, but in hopes of a new community. Society cannot tolerate this claim that there can be something better, so it emphasizes the despair and belittles the hope as delusional. Suicide is an attack on society—an attack on its omnipotence, on its denial of death, and on its own despair.

Psychology agrees with society, but adds the somewhat obvious thought that suicide is an attack on the self. As Karl Menninger puts it, there is both a wish to kill and a wish to be killed.[10] The dynamic is given in a New Yorker cartoon of some time ago.

The cartoon represents in the first picture, a man sitting despondently beside the picture of a woman, a revolver held in his right hand. In the subsequent pictures he first raises the revolver and places it at his temple with an air of resignation. Then a thought seems to strike him and he lowers the revolver, while he takes another look at the picture of the woman. In the final picture he has thrown back his head and, pointing the revolver at the picture of the woman, fires, blowing the picture to bits while an air of triumph and satisfaction mingles with his evident anger.[11]

The dynamic is also revealed by a patient of Menninger who had many heart attacks and had been told by a competent physician that he had two years at most to live. In the course of psychological treatment, it was discovered that he had lost the woman he loved to a man who had been his best friend. There was tremendous resentment against this man, to whom he could not express it. For several weeks before the heart attacks began he had struggled secretly with a desire to strangle his friend for this betrayal. In the end he sought psychotherapy, and it was successful. The attacks stopped. Ten years later the patient was still well, happily married, and at the height of his creative powers. Hate had begun to destroy the body, but was removed before the damage could be permanent.

So psychology says that the attack is also on the self. The

concern of psychotherapists and the creation of prevention centers make it clear that such an attack is to be prevented. Psychology tends to condemn the act. Since it does not as yet have the power to enforce justice, it relies on scientific labels. Modern psychologists do make a great point of saying that insanity is a rather infrequent cause of suicide. But one reason they are able to say this is because a new term is available. Rather than "insane" or "psychotic," they attach the label of "neurotic." Then they quickly repeat all that was formerly said under the category of insanity—magical act, illogical thinking, and delusions. Ther term is different, but the odor is the same: one who attempts suicide is sick. Psychology sees suicide as an attack on the self and frequently condemns it by defamation of character.

What really bothers psychologists about suicide? It is not just a matter of aggression and guilt, of the wish to kill and be killed. People seek release from unendurable situations. It is a matter of what Menninger calls the wish to die.[12] For Menninger, conscious disgust or weariness of life joins hand with an unconscious death instinct to produce a desire for death. There is not only aggression and guilt, but a wish to come to an end. But why? Primary masochism? This is a most modern hypothesis created out of despair of understanding. Until modern times, what every Tom, Dick, and Harry has known is that you come to an end in order to come to a new beginning. Current research indicates that "the idea of making a new start by destroying the old (bad) self" seems known mostly by children and schizophrenics.[13] Of course these two groups of human beings are by definition irresponsible. It is interesting that although psychology has learned more from children and psychotics than from any other source, it continues to only note in passing and summarily dismiss this theme of rebirth. Possibly this is because psychology is so embedded in culture that it can only pursue adjustment to what it is, and so we have the Freudian goal of achieving everyday misery and the Adlerian goal of cooperation. It may be that the prevailing focus on self-understanding is so dynamically opposed to focus on drastic change of self that one prohibits the other. Or perhaps the goal of self-understanding is a covert counsel of despair: no change is possible, no cause is realistic, therefore let us make honesty the goal. Whatever the reasoning here, psychology minimizes what may be crucial for our understanding. The suicide does attack the self, not just out of aggression, guilt, and the desire to die, but out of hope of discovering a new self. This amounts to an attack on much of contemporary psychology as well.

Theology sees suicide as an attack on God. Condemnation by Christianity has always prevailed. The commandment evoked is: "Thou shalt not kill." Augustine claimed that the commandment meant just what it said, that it cannot be modified by restating it as "Thou shalt not kill *others.*" According to Thomas Aquinas, suicide is "the most fatal of sins because it cannot be repented of." A suicide is traditionally deprived of ecclesiastical burial in the Roman Church, and Protestants have responded in identical fashion; John Wesley proposed that the naked bodies of female suicides be dragged through the streets. The most common reasoning of the theologians seems to be that since God created our lives, they are not ours to do with as we please. We are his creatures, and to willfully choose our deaths is a denial of our creatureliness. Only God reigns over life and death, so it follows that suicide is a monstrous attempt to take over the throne. Sin is rebellion against God and suicide is an attack on him.

What really bothers theology about suicide? It is not only a matter of usurping God's reign over life and death. It may be granted that sin is involved, just as it is involved in much other human behavior. It is an attack on God just as all our behavior as sinners is an attack. But the typical attitude of theology raises a question. It seems to be that death must come from without, from war, accident, or disease. Of course God may be seen as working through these events. In some inscrutable way, they are signs of his will. Yet God is being forbidden by theology to work his will from within the individual. Why cannot God work in this particular mysterious way? Can it be that the suicide's hope of a new community and new self assumes a hope which is not really present in theology? The suicide may not want to destroy the life given by God. He may want to destroy the life given by Satan, the life given over to the power of sin. He desires to destroy the life which leads to death. It is the life given by God which he has lost and hopes to regain. The suicide is a sinner who attacks God, but he may be also a child of God who is attacking the god of theologians.

These questions are raised about the reactions of society, psychology, and theology not to dismiss but to deepen them. Suicide is a problem, and it is an act of behavior to be prevented. It goes against society, the self, and God. But because it may have its source in the hope for a new community, new self and new relationship to God it may be something more. *Suicide is an attack on transformation.*

The term "attack" has two different meanings. The primary definition is: to fall upon with violence. The secondary definition is: to set to work upon with vigor. Insofar as suicide is a setting to work upon the task of transformation with vigor, it is spiritually legitimate. But insofar as it approaches this task with violence, it is illegitimate. Both probably apply in nearly all cases of suicide, but the element of violence operates throughout. Suicide is a problem because it is a travesty on the rites of transformation.

Our society has lost the spiritual wisdom which provided ritual means for death and rebirth within life itself. But there are individuals who discover this wisdom on their own. We become possessed by a vague, largely unconscious realization that something drastic must happen. The adversities of life engender an urge for rebirth, through the death of what is intolerable. Contemporary culture cannot perceive this need at all clearly, tends not to approve it, and is quite unable to offer any creative guidance. But the urge will not go away. So the individual is *isolated* by his new hope. On the one hand, this isolation serves to increase the suicide's attack on society, self, and God. On the other hand, the isolation prevents development in the individual of the budding wisdom of death and rebirth. Consequently, a travesty of the real spirit of it occurs. The new wisdom is so primitive within him, as in the child and the psychotic, that three erroneous things take place. First, the act is too *hasty*. In a sense, suicide is not premature death; on the contrary, death of the old self has been overdelayed—the act is an attempt to make up for lost time. But transformation does not occur in this way. The actual rite is always preceded by careful initiation and orientation. The suicide's lack of caution leads to superficial action. Second, the act of suicide is too *assaultive*. It is an attempt to *force* a rebirth by literally storming the gates of death. Rebirth is a gift, and one cannot be grabby about it. Third—perhaps most tragic of all—by never getting beyond the primitive level the suicide remains literalistic. Transformation of life is equated unconsciously with transformation of the body. The result is coming to an end rather than to a beginning. Thus destructive collaboration between our society and its members reduces a spiritual necessity to a magical act.

If suicide is a mystery to us, it is because we are in some degree the living dead, those who have forgotten our need for rebirth. By contrast, the suicide is still capable of action, however perverted. Put yourself firmly into your own shoes and consider the circumstances and motivations for your own suicide.

1. If you did commit suicide sometime, what would be the most likely circumstances?

Aggression or rejection by others	____
Physical illness or pain	____
Fear of insanity or senility	____
Failure	____
Loneliness or loss of a loved one	____
Family conflict	____
Other (be brief)	_____

2. If you did commit suicide sometime, what would be the
   most likely wish?
   　　　　Wish to kill   ——
   　　　　Wish to be killed   ——
   　　　　Wish to die   ——
   　　　　Wish to be reborn   ——
   　　　　Other (be brief) _____

Current opposition between the living dead and the suicide
prevents the action you have contemplated, yet fails to foster
rebirth. What we require is an understanding of *successful*
suicide—that is, a suicide within life, in a manner of speaking
—and the means of achieving it.

Prevention by Permission

Given the understanding of suicide as a travesty of the deep
impulse toward transformation, what should be the nature of a
preventative attitude?

Suicide can be prevented only by permitting it. Knowledge
of the art of dying within life must be rediscovered and applied.
This is the concern of the remaining exercises; the concluding
remarks are only a preliminary.

The Jungian analyst James Hillman, in *Suicide and the Soul,*
offers astute advice on the nature of the responsibility of a
counselor and on the nature of the strategy involved. With
regard to responsibility, Hillman claims: "We are not responsible for one another's lives or deaths; each man's life and death
is his own. But we are responsible to our involvements."[14] The
suicidal individual is a threat to both the psychological and the
religious professional. More than anything else, he is a threat to
our feelings of omnipotence. A feeling of helplessness is legitimate, but a sense of failure and guilt when a counselee commits
suicide is sometimes unreasonable and vain. The attempt to
control a suicidal human being in order to prevent bodily death

may be another sign of assumed omnipotence. Furthermore, it is unwise. Like the suicidal person, one becomes overconcerned about the body and confirms his primitive understanding. What we are responsible for is the individual's spiritual life. The cry for help from the suicide does mean help me live, but also, help me die. We must not cheat him of his desire for the experience of death as our society tends to do. Our responsibility is to help him discover the meaningfulness of death; this means to remove the haste, assault, and literalistic aspects of his goal, so that the death experience can create a new life. Our task is to provide the experience of death *before* physical death occurs. Thus suicide is prevented by permitting it to occur in a different way.

Concerning the strategy involved in prevention by permission. Hillman writes:

> The more the impulse towards suicide is conscious, the more it will tend to color all psychic life with despair. And the more this despair can be held, the less the suicide will "just happen." To hope for nothing, to expect nothing, to demand nothing. This is analytical despair. To entertain no false hopes, not even that hope for relief which brings one into analysis in the first place. This is an emptiness of soul and will. It is the condition present from that hour when, for the first time, the patient feels there is no hope at all for getting better, or even for changing, whatsoever. An analysis leads up to this moment and by constellating this despair lets free the suicidal impulse. Upon this moment of truth, the whole work depends, because this is the dying away from the false life and wrong hopes out of which the complaint has come. As it is the moment of truth, it is also the moment of despair, because there is no hope.[15]

Hillman is saying that we should not try to give the ego support by building up its hopes, prescribing medical remedies, or dispensing superficial consolations. We are to stop treating the individual as a patient who can be cured. We give up our own hope for the individual. By so doing, we become able to accept the individual's own experience. Then, in the keeping of a kind of death vigil together, the panic reaction diminishes, and with it the hasty assault on death. At this point there is time and space to consider life and death and to discover the seeds of a new community, a new self, and a new relation to God. Man has always known that true transformation never begins until one reaches the point of absolutely no hope—the "sickness unto death." It is the task of the counselor to help the counselee reach this point. This is prevention of suicide by permission.

To some extent we are all committing suicide and experiencing death in life. We are like the young man who narrates Melville's tale of death, *Moby Dick*. He muses at the beginning:

Call me Ishmael. Some years ago—never mind how long precisely—having little or no money in my purse, and nothing particular to interest me on shore, I thought I would sail about a little and see the watery part of the world. It is a way I have of driving off the spleen, and regulating the circulation. Whenever I find myself growing grim around the mouth; whenever it is a damp, drizzly November in my soul; whenever I find myself involuntarily pausing before coffin warehouses, and bringing up the rear of every funeral I meet; and especially whenever my hypos get such an upper hand of me, that it requires a strong moral principle to prevent me from deliberately stepping into the street, and methodically knocking people's hats off—then, I account it high time to get to sea as soon as I can. This is my substitute for pistol and ball. With a philosophical flourish Cato throws himself upon his sword; I quietly take to the ship.[16]

Ishmael has no attachments to others, is depressed, angry, and wants to leave—to leave life. He is a suitable narrator for a story whose hero, Captain Ahab, is so despairingly and angrily seeking death. Ishmael takes to the ship of death, and he only escapes to tell the tale. He is extraordinarily lucky. We may not be so. Yet the destruction we bring on ourselves has a kernel of spiritual value. We are not only attacking society, ourselves, and God, but are also—somehow—getting to work at transformation. Like Ishmael, we have the opportunity to visit death and return from the dead to a new life. If the art of dying within life can be mastered, both the magical act of suicide and the magical act of suicide prevention will be overcome.

The following exercises on grief, belief, and martyrdom are constructed to assist us in successful suicide—a death that leads to rebirth.

Transformation by Grief

"Man, when he does not grieve, almost ceases to exist." True or not, this is a depressing thought. We would prefer not to grieve just as we would prefer not to die. "Blessed are those who mourn: for they shall be comforted." So we affirm, but the comfort rarely seems sufficient and sometimes it is absent. Chekov portrays our mood.

Here, in the bedroom, dead quiet reigned. Everything, down to the last trifle, spoke eloquently of the tempest undergone, of weariness, and everything rested. The candle which stood among a close crowd of phials, boxes and jars on the stool and the big lamp on the chest of drawers brightly lit the room. On the bed, by the window, the boy lay open-eyed, with a look of wonder on his face. He did not move, but it seemed that his open eyes became darker and darker every second and sank into his skull. Having laid her hands on his body and hid her face in the folds of the bedclothes, the mother now was on her knees before the bed. Like the boy she did not move, but how much living movement was felt in the coil of her body and in her hands! She was pressing close to the bed with her whole being, with eager vehemence, as though she were not afraid to violate the quiet and comfortable post which she had found at last for her weary body. Blankets, cloths, basins, splashes on the floor, brushes and spoons scattered everywhere, a white bottle of lime-water, the stifling heavy air itself—everything died away, and as it were plunged into quietude. . . . The doctor stopped by his wife, thrust his hands into his trouser pockets and bending his head on one side looked fixedly at his son. His face showed indifference; only the drops which glistened on his beard revealed that he had been lately weeping. . . . The repulsive terror of which we think when we speak of death was absent from the bedroom. In the pervading dumbness, in the mother's pose, in the indifference of the doctor's face was something attractive that touched the heart, the subtle and elusive beauty of human grief, which it will take men long to understand and describe, and only music, it seems, is able to express. Beauty too was felt in the stern stillness. Kirilov and his wife were silent and did not weep, as though they confessed all the poetry of their condition. As once the season of their youth passed away, so now in this boy their right to bear children passed away, alas! for ever to eternity. The doctor is forty-four years old, already grey and looks an old man; his faded sick wife is thirty-five. Andrey was not merely the only son but the last.[1]

In this picture we see quiet, weariness, sorrow, and indifference—and most of all loss: the loss of a son and many other losses. Yet Chekov attempts to indicate something else as well, although he obliquely confesses his inability to do so by affirming that only music can communicate his thoughts. There is a beauty in grief; indeed, a grandeur. Perhaps "comfort" is a misleading term for the positive aspects of grief.

Thus far we have considered our own death by looking at our denial, our fear, and our death in life. Now we come to the question of grief, and will follow it presently by considering belief and new life. But we have not arrived at grief only just now. Whenever death is mentioned, grief reactions occur. During the earlier exercises, we responded with grief. It is an experience composed of many elements, and we have already been exposing ourselves to the negative ones. And to consider beliefs and new life will not be leaving aside grief but exploring the positive elements. So we are at a central point, a time of gestation, which includes recollection of what has gone before and anticipation of what is to come. Grief is the subject of the total exercise in which we are engaged.

We shall examine our own grief in three ways. We will explore first, our reactions to the death of someone close to us—the task of the bereaved; second, the reactions of a contemporary adult who dies of cancer—the task of the dying; and third, the reactions of a primitive child who dies a different kind of death—the task of everyman. By looking at these deaths of others, we may be able to see our own death out of the corner of our eye. Actually, more than perception is required. The grief process is death and birth. We are to die—now.

Task of the Bereaved

We begin with what is most familiar to us. When a death in our family occurs, we experience a variety of reactions that are symptoms of grief. So we take our first look at the death of another by looking at our reactions and at what happens to them. These have been noted by Erich Lindemann in his classic study, "Symptomatology and Management of Acute Grief."[2]

We are familiar with three kinds of reactions: physical, emotional, and behavioral. Some of our reactions are physical. These include a feeling of tightness in the throat, shortness of breath, and choking. There is a common complaint about weariness and exhaustion. The stomach feels hollow and food loses its taste. More than this, we often have a perceptual sense of unreality. Other people may actually appear to be farther away from us than they are; they may appear small or dark. And there is generally an intense preoccupation with the image of the deceased, sometimes to the extent of experiencing an hallucination. At the end of the movie *Love is a Many-Splendored Thing*, the heroine climbs up a hill where she met her lover before he died. As she nears the top, she sees him for a brief moment coming toward her as he did when alive. Such hallucinations are probably quite common, although too frightening to be commonly acknowledged.

We also have feeling reactions. There is usually sorrow over the loss. There may be relief that prolonged agony is finished. And there may even be joy in remembrance of the quality of the deceased's life. But we also feel guilty and angry. We search ourselves for all the mistakes we made before the death. "Why did I fail to——? If I had only known—— If I could do it over again——" Previously hidden feelings of guilt are let loose into consciousness, and past known guilt is increased. And guilt may be a result of earlier hostility toward the deceased. Sometimes this element of anger may be clearly observed, but more frequently antagonism is directed toward the living—the relatives, friends, and professionals who are trying to be helpful.

Along with these physical and emotional changes, we experience a marked inability to carry on the habits of customary living. We may be active. Indeed, we often are quite restless and constantly on the search for something to do. But the bustle in the house has no zest. We are simply going through the motions. Much of our daily activity was intimately related to the deceased; now it has lost its meaning. There is no motivation for our usual patterns of behavior. We lament:

> Listen, children:
> Your father is dead.
> From his old coats
> I'll make you little jackets;
> I'll make you little trousers
> From his old pants.
> There'll be in his pockets
> Things he used to put there,
> Keys and pennies
> Covered with tobacco;
> Dan shall have the pennies
> To save in his bank;
> Anne shall have the keys
> To make a pretty noise with.
> Life must go on,
> Though good men die;

Anne, eat your breakfast;
Dan, take your medicine;
Life must go on;
I forget just why.[3]

Although these symptoms are experienced in private loneli-
ness, they are actually highly social phenomena. One social
complication occurs because contemporary dying *takes time.* If
death occurs suddenly by accident, grief begins after death. But
this does not always happen. Dying can take months and even
years. Glaser and Strauss outline the process in their list of
"critical junctures:"

(1) The patient is defined as dying. (2) Staff and family then make
preparations for his death, as he may do himself if he knows he is dying.
(3) At some point, there seems to be "nothing more to do" to prevent
death. (4) The final descent may take weeks, or days, or merely hours,
ending in (5) the "last hours," (6) the death watch, and (7) the death
itself.[4]

Clearly, bereavement can begin before the death of a loved
one. And the attitude of the bereaved may conflict with that of
the one who is dying. Either may deny while the other acknowledges death. The one who is to survive may resent the burden
of care for the dying and have to deal with hostility and guilt
as a consequence. The survivor may go through the grief process before death and turn toward new relationships, actually
abandoning the dying. Or the dying may loosen their ties to the
living before the living are able to comprehend this natural
withdrawal. Such anticipatory bereavement and its consequences are complex and may make the ensuing bereavement
after the death even more complex.

A second social complication is custom. Grief occurs in the
context not only of a family, but also of a culture. Within every
culture, subculture, and to a certain extent every extended
family, there are expectations as to what is appropriate. Who
should grieve and who should not? Is the spouse to be equally

or more or less stricken than the parents? Is the loss to be suffered more by the maternal side or the paternal side of the extended family? How visible should sorrow be? Very visible or quite invisible? Visible in women and invisible in men? What other emotions are permitted? Can hate and joy be shown? When is mourning to end—immediately after the funeral, after several months, after a year, or never? When is remarriage appropriate—as soon as possible (as in some primitive groups), after a year, or never? There can be quite different answers to these questions within the family, within the extended family, and between the family and the community. In our pluralistic society such clashes are likely because of different expectations. The gathering of a family and community at the time of death does not necessarily fulfill our individual and group need for social cohesiveness.

Our reactions to a death in the family can be either creative or destructive. When the latter occurs, symptoms are prolonged and powerful. There may be extreme physical reactions which possibly lead to such psychosomatic conditions as asthma, ulcerative colitis, or rheumatoid arthritis; extreme guilt which fosters chronic depression and suicide; extreme hostility which prompts antisocial behavior; or that extreme isolation which is psychosis. It is unfinished grief over loss that fosters death in life. And it is our capacity to conclude grief that offers the possibility of discovering new life in the midst of death. For our grief to be creative, we have to complete a specific task. This is our central concern and we shall explore it in several contexts.

The nature of the task can be stated simply. Our basic response to the crisis of death is a resounding No. This must be transformed into a Yes to death. But this transformation entails a No to life. So the second No must be transformed into a Yes. We begin with a No to death, proceed to a Yes to death, involving No to life, and end with a Yes to both death and life. There are two transformations required, movements from the No to death and the No to life to affirmation of both.

Of course what can be so simply put, cannot be so simply achieved. The living respond to death with a No. What is our response when we hear that someone has died—what do we actually say? It is often that simple ejaculation, "No!" Or we say, "Why, that couldn't be!" Or we protest, "But I saw him just yesterday!"—meaning that since he was alive twenty-four hours ago he must be alive now. When someone dies our immediate reaction is denial. Those who remain in shock and maintain the denial are only superficially attached to life, by means of an illusion. To live permanently in this stage is to be one of the dead in life.

At best, it takes time for full significance of a loss to be recognized. A tradition that helps certify the reality of death is that of preparing the corpse for burial. When a body is handled, our primitive senses of touch and smell send a message difficult to ignore. Even though "viewing the remains" in a funeral home does not appeal to some, it *can* serve to enforce acceptance of the reality of death. And our tendency to tell the story of the deceased's illness and death over and over again eventually brings further awareness that what we are telling has actually happened.

This physical and intellectual acceptance of death is not sufficient. As the reality of the loss becomes apparent, sorrow will increase. Guilt and hostility will follow. All these feelings, whether or not socially appropriate, need to be ventilated or handled in some way that prevents a return to denial. Family, friends, and professionals should not halt this expression by their cautions or premature assurances. Such prohibition is primarily for one's own sake—not the bereaved. Man can endure cursing (although he cannot take it very well). Life per se can take it. And God can take it. The ancient practices of wailing, beating the breast, and tearing the hair served the individual by perserving communication between men, between men and God, and between men and death. In our society we need more freedom to express ourselves. And perhaps we need free-

dom *not* to express feelings that are not really ours. To some
degree, we are like the woman in Ambrose Bierce's fantastic
fable, "The Devoted Widow."

A Widow weeping on her husband's grave was approached by an
Engaging Gentleman who, in a respectful manner, assured her that he
had long entertained for her the most tender feelings.

"Wretch!" cried the Widow. "Leave me this instant! Is this a time to
talk to me of love?"

"I assure you, madam, that I had not intended to disclose my affec-
tion," the Engaging Gentleman humbly explained, "but the power of
your beauty has overcome my discretion."

"You should see me when I have not been weeping," said the
Widow.[5]

This physical, intellectual, and emotional acceptance of death
is a transformation of our No into a Yes. Then we discover our
second No. The event of a death has taken us out of the everyday world. Life has become a tale "told by an idiot, full of sound
and fury, signifying nothing." To this life we say No. One individual, speaking about his reactions to the death of his wife, put
the matter succinctly: "The first decision one has to make is this:
Is he going to continue to live, or is he going to take his own
life?" This is the basic question. For in some sense the tendency
is to commit suicide. The bereaved kills himself either by taking
his life, or by allowing himself to be ruled by his memories,
living in the past. In either case, he holds hands with the dead
and lives among them quite disconnected from life. To continue permanently in this stage is to be one of the dead in
life.

It can be understood why primitive peoples feared the dead,
sent them on long journeys, and exorcised their ghosts out of
the community. Otherwise they would not have been able to
get on with their daily work. So most societies have tended to
have a definite mourning period with a precise end at which
time the bereaved was required to conclude his grief. Many of

us lack such ritual aids today. And our supreme and nearly idolatrous reliance on the nuclear family does not make our task any easier. But the goal is to return to the world of the living, to say Yes to life while maintaining our Yes to death. Movement to this total acceptance is completion of the process of grief. The result is a new level of living with increased understanding and appreciation of existence. Unending bereavement is living death, whereas completion is the beginning of a new life that is far more creative than the old one.

It is appropriate at this point in the exercise to count our own losses and their costs. Each one of us has grieved, and some of us still do.

1. List the three most significant losses you have sustained. These could be losses of people, things, hopes, or something else. Be brief and concrete.

   _____

   _____

   _____

2. In which of the three losses have you completed your grief? In what ways has this completion moved you to more creative living? Be brief and be concrete.

3. In which of the three losses have you failed to complete your grief? In what ways has this incompletion crippled your living? Be brief and be concrete.

Task of the Dying

Thus far this exercise has presented a reminder of our reactions to the loss of a loved one and an outline of the task of the bereaved. Now the focus shifts to the dying person himself. The purpose is to apply our experience and understanding of bereavement to one who is going to die and knows it.

The poet Rilke said of the patients in a Paris hospital:

This excellent hotel is very ancient. Even in King Clovis' time people died in it in a number of beds. Now they are dying there in 559 beds. Factory-like, of course. Where production is so enormous an individual death is not so nicely carried out; but then that doesn't matter. It is quantity that counts. Who cares anything today for a finely-finished death? No one. Even the rich, who could after all afford this luxury of dying in full detail, are beginning to be careless and indifferent; the wish to have a death of one's own is growing ever rarer. . . . One dies just as it comes; one dies the death that belongs to the disease one has (for since one has come to know all the diseases, one knows, too, that the different lethal terminations belong to the disease and not to the people; and the sick person has, so to speak, nothing to do).[6]

Rilke complains that we die like animals, or even like vegetables. The modern hospital becomes a bizarre hotel containing people who are relieved of physical and emotional pain—and of their humanity as well. Some people do not really die any more, they just fade away.

Investigation by current psychologists and psychiatrists suggests that a human death is possible. Elisabeth Kubler-Ross indicates that patients can be helped to pass through the stages of denial and isolation, anger, bargaining, and depression to acceptance and hope.[7] Progressions through these stages are not as smooth as an outline tends to suggest. And formulation of such detailed stages occurs as much for the sake of the theoretician as for the sake of the patient. Yet the conception of a path to follow does provide an orientation which helps staff and patient recognize and work toward a human death. A more humble and equally useful guide is provided by Weisman and Hackett in their important essay, "Predilection to Death." They conclude:

An appropriate attitude toward death . . . comes about when (1) there is quiet acceptance that death is a solution to abiding problems, or that few problems remain at the time of death; (2) superego demands are reduced; (3) optimal interpersonal relations are maintained; and (4) the ego is encouraged to operate at as high a level as may be compatible with the physical illness.[8]

Both these examples indicate a professional realization that there is something to do for and with the dying. It is probably this attitude rather than our limited wisdom that makes a difference to the patient.

Because not all have had intimate contact with one who is going to die and knows it, our discussion begins with data provided by Charles Wertenbaker.[9] He was a writer and an editor of *Time* magazine, with a wife and two children, and died of cancer in 1955. His story sufficiently reveals his faults: too much pride, a great deal of pettiness, and on occasion an unreasonable amount of anger. But it also reveals his struggle to live by principles, and one of these was to die like a man.

When Wertenbaker suspected that the tender lump in his abdomen was cancerous, he contemplated swimming out into the ocean near his home, looking back and remembering for the last time, and then filling his lungs with water. He said: "The alternative was hospitals, pain, becoming a patient instead of a person, and probably the same result in the end—only by then I would be reduced to something less than a man who could swim out to meet his death." When his suspicion was confirmed by a doctor, he decided to take that swim. The following morning, he left instructions concerning his papers and went to the beach. In his datebook for that day, he wrote: "No swim." Among the reasons for this change of mind was the issue of pain. He had suffered little physical pain during his life and felt that to avoid it would now be cowardly. To face it would be a test of manhood.

Immediately the Wertenbakers traveled to a hospital for an exploratory operation. He pledged his wife to tell him the truth about his chance for life and about the possible amount of time that might be left. The doctors concluded after the operation that he might live for about three months at most. They used all the pressure they could muster to prevent his being told. She refused to remove his dignity by telling a lie. At the very moment that he regained consciousness, the man was told. He smiled at his wife and went back to sleep.

After Wertenbaker recovered from the immediate operation, they returned home. Against the better judgment of the doctors of course. And as they faced the truth themselves, they also revealed it to many of their friends and neighbors. Old friends came to renew their friendship and to pay their respects to the living *before he died.* A close friend, John Hersey, was moved to say to him: "You make me want to write. . . . We love you truly and you live in us truly and forever."

During these last months of life, Charles Wertenbaker remained in character—proud, petty, angry, demanding. Once he wrote: "Last Sunday to Sunday. The week out. . . . The week we almost lost each other. I had become a patient." But he remained in character in other ways as well. His son had previously begun to teach him how to play the guitar. These lessons continued. And when he died, the son was pleased that his father had learned a new song. Along with this play with his children and talks with his wife, was work at his trade. He began to write a short book which was to be called, *Sixty Days in a Lifetime.* It was to contain his autobiography, his experience of dying and this thoughts on life and death. So Wertenbaker lived out his last days in a rather prosaic fashion with no urge to do something different.

But there was a difference. His appreciation of daily experiences increased—the sound of Bach, the taste of food, the feel of sand and wind. He looked inward, reviewing and evaluating himself and his relations with others. He looked outward, and his love ripened. There was a difference. He was very glad that he had not taken the swim in the ocean. Near the end, he wrote a note to himself on a scrap of paper. He said: "Hit hard on swim refusal—I'd have drowned the best part of my life."

Charles Wertenbaker died on January 7, 1955. The doctors had wanted to take him to the hospital for another operation which would not save but would prolong his life. He declined, not wanting to spend his last days in an institution. When, in time, he was physically disabled, unable to eat, and incapable of writing, the man and his wife decided that he should die. She aided him in the act of suicide. She said to him: "I love you— I love you—— Please die." He said, "I love you," and then he died.

The death of this man is hardly commendable in detail. He had all sorts of problems in human relations. He held no traditional religious beliefs. His suicide, although it cut short his life by only a few days, is not an act for all to follow. Nor should our hospitals be abandoned. But Charles Wertenbaker did *die*. He did not just fade away. He refused to be deprived of his death, and died like the man he was. It was a "finely-finished death."

How did this death come about? The answer is in the form of a simple proposition. *The task of the bereaved is also the task of the dying.* This means two things. First, it means that the individual who knows or senses that he is dying is also himself bereaved. All the physical symptoms of grief may appear. There may be feelings of guilt and hostility. There is guilt due to intense awareness of past failures, and of present failures as a person who is dying. There is hostility over past and present mistreatment, especially over the very common abandonment of the dying by the living. And there are both hostility and guilt arising out of the perception that others will continue to live. Finally, there will be withdrawal from the world. The old daily patterns will not be meaningful. The dying will retreat into preoccupation with the past. So the first point is that Charles Wertenbaker was the bereaved himself, as are all who are aware of their dying.

The second point is that those who suffer their own loss have the same task as those who suffer the loss of someone else. The dying face the challenge of transforming the No to death and the No to life into affirmations. Wertenbaker made these two movements. He turned his denial of death into acceptance.

Suicide is committed sometimes to deny death. If he had filled his lungs with water at the beginning, he would have been running away, eliminating his fears by destroying himself along with them. But he did not. He accepted his death and forced his wife, his community, and his friends to accept it also. Rarely, if ever, can death be truly faced privately. We prefer to fool ourselves. It is in sharing this reality with others that it can be accepted. And Wertenbaker expressed his feelings about his own death. They were not all positive, but he ventilated them by talking with his wife and friends and by writing about them. Thus they became meaningful to him and useful to others. His No to death became a Yes.

Wertenbaker completed the second part of the task of the bereaved by reinvesting himself in the world. To him the hospital may have served as a symbol for withdrawal, a place where he might do as so many others have done—turn his face to the wall and whimper until transformed into an animal or vegetable. There were times of withdrawal during his last months, but he returned from them to enter fully into his life and serve his family and friends. His No to life became a Yes.

This possibility of growth in human relationships coupled with a meaningful death appears to be challenged in a provocative essay by C. Knight Aldrich. He affirms that

it is particularly difficult for the strong, well-integrated personality to accept with equanimity the idea of his own death. For example, a man with many friends, solid accomplishments, a devout belief in a benign hereafter, and successful adaptation to a permanent disability, was informed that he suffered from an incurable carcinoma. At first he was profoundly depressed, although he was able successfully to conceal his depression from his friends and relatives; later, he managed to persuade himself that he was recovering in spite of symptomatic evidence to the contrary and in spite of his physicians' well-meaning attempts to set him right. His friends and relatives, apparently in an effort to maintain their image of the patient as a "realistic" personality, in turn denied the evidence of both his earlier depression and his later denial, insisting that he had faced his problem courageously and without depression to the end. Thus his friends' use of denial served to perpetuate the belief that the "strong" personality faces death with equanimity. . . . Strength of personality may help a patient not so much to avoid depression in anticipation of death as to conceal depression from others. . . . The more personality resources a person has, the more friends he has and the closer are his relationships with them; the more friends and close relationships, the more grief; and all things be equal, the more grief, the more suffering.[10]

The initial points Aldrich makes are valid. Ego strength does allow the concealment of affect from loved ones. Relatives will see just what they can afford to see, and will idealize as well. But Aldrich also claims that the more love, the more suffering. This is disputable. Aldrich does not indicate what he is referring to by the phrase, "all things being equal." Sense of loss will increase as the depth of human relationships increases. But hostility, guilt and despair will decrease if relationships are harmonized. A pure sense of loss is hardly the same as that which is embedded in these other emotions. It is the latter that are so destructive and lead to so much suffering. When a relationship grows and develops, as it did in the last days of Wertenbaker, the destructive elements of living and dying do not get in the way of either. The ego will narrow its boundaries toward the end and let go of relationships to others. Wertenbaker's decision to die is such a retraction of the ego. But this occurred precisely because of reconciliation and establishment of love, rather than lack of interest in others. Love makes letting go possible.

Charles Wertenbaker completed the task of the bereaved. And he discovered what others have discovered: completion of the task leads to a higher level of living. He did not become an animal or vegetable, but gained a new life. As a result, the time of his dying was a time of receiving and giving meaning and joy more than ever before. He was one man who cared for a "finely-finished death," and he achieved it.

Task of Everyman

As we have seen, grief may come into being before or after death. The first sort, anticipatory grief, may refer to the death of another or to one's own. If the latter, it may be divided heuristically into four types. In the first, death is perceived as *near* and *certain*. The terminal cancer patient may be well aware that death will occur within weeks or days or even hours. In the second type of anticipatory grief, death is perceived as *near and uncertain*. Some heart patients will know that death is not inevitable but surely an immediate possibility. Those participating in such dangerous work as mining or war may also see their own death in this fashion. In the third type, death is perceived as *distant* and *certain*. Death surely will occur, but probably not for a long time to come. This is a prevalent theme of philosophers and a possible perception for anyone who indeed acknowledges that the fact of death, along with taxes, is the one thing man knows for sure. In the fourth type of anticipatory grief, death is perceived as *distant* and *uncertain*. This is the awareness that death will not occur for a long time to come and perhaps not even then. Examination of observable human behavior and not-so-observable human fantasy suggests that this type is exceedingly prevalent. Man tends to lead a life of quiet desperation in which anticipatory grief is covert and open wonder about death negligible.

Thus far in this exercise, it has been claimed that the task of those who have suffered a loss in the family is to transform their No to death, and life into acceptance. And it has been suggested that the task of the dying is identical. The discussion may have been relevant to those of us who still mourn the loss of someone who has died, and to those of us who have reason to mourn our own death in the near future. For the rest of us, those who have not sustained a significant loss and have statistical expectations of a great number of years ahead, grief is anticipatory over a death that is distant and certain. We are all terminal. Indeed, it may be remarked that we are all terminally ill. The religious response to this universal situation is *initiatory grief*. It is visible in contemporary religious practices, but most clearly seen in primitive religions. The following discussion will examine very removed and somewhat extreme behavior in order to highlight a basic religious perception.

We look at another death, a different kind of death: the death, within the life cycle, of a primitive child. The purpose is to refine our understanding of the task of the bereaved and to perceive it as the task for everyone. The child is a boy of ten years of age and a member of a primitive tribe in Australia. He is about to pass through a puberty rite which has three states: death, gestation, and rebirth.[11]

After the older men have prepared a sacred space in the bush, a mother brings her son to the edge of the village. She does not know the content of the rite. She has heard only rumors about death and manhood. She does know that, occasionally, a child fails to return. The little boy knows the same. Both are filled with excitement and pride, but also with anxiety. The men rush forward and tear the boy away from his mother. She weeps and wails over his forthcoming death. The boy is taken to a hut where he lies down on his back with his arms crossed over his chest. He is covered with a mat and told not to utter a sound. During the coming days, he may be symbolically burned by a fire, buried in a shallow pit or ritually dismembered. All these things—separation from mother, darkness, silence, physical dangers—are experiences of death. The boy is told that the god or gods are killing him. He does not know for sure whether he will survive or not. Occasionally the dangerous rite does kill a child. So this first stage of the puberty rite is one of death. The child's self and the child's world are destroyed.

The second part of the ritual takes place over an extended period of time. The boy meets his god and receives his name.

After this he may have to be fed by a guardian for as long as six months. Newborn infants cannot feed themselves. During this time he is instructed and trained to meditate on his experience. By means of dance, pantomine, and myth he is introduced to the gods, to the history of the tribe, and to the way he is to live. This second stage of the puberty rite is one of gestation. A new self and new world have been impregnated and nourished.

In the final part of the rite, the boy is returned to the community to take his place as a new person in a new world. The boy and his mother do not acknowledge each other for some time. Her *son* has died. It is a strange man who has entered the village. And the boy does not know his mother. He does know the ways of adults and the ways of the gods. The old self and the old world have been transformed. The boy has been reborn.

Using our previous understanding, we discover that this rite provides an occasion for grief and for completion of the task of the bereaved. It seems sufficiently clear that the rite prompts our typical physical, emotional, and behavioral reactions to death. And it seems equally clear that it demands acceptance of death and acceptance of life. This understanding gives us clues about both the *nature* and the *timing* of grief.

The first clue concerns the nature of anticipatory grief. Major religious rites are responses to the crises of life. A crisis is an event which raises the issue of survival. Events of passage, such as coming of age, marriage, and death are crises. They are met by rites of initiation. The religious response is that man must die. The natural threat of death is met by a spiritual demand for the death that precedes rebirth.

So what is the task of the bereaved? *It is to die* and be reborn. Whether grief strikes the survivors or the dying, their task is to die. Their lives are threatened. The appropriate response is to transform this natural threat into a spiritual reality. A grieving survivor finds his world destroyed by the loss of a loved one. His task is to complete the destruction. He is to kill what little remains of his world and to kill himself as well. A dying and grieving person finds himself about to be destroyed. His task is to complete the destruction. He is to kill what little remains of himself and to kill the old world as well. In either case, the old self and the old world are destroyed. This is what is involved in perceiving and accepting death. It is the active destruction of what little remains of what has been. Death is perceived and accepted only by dying. Then rebirth can occur. The old self, the old world, and all our memories of them are transformed for service of our present and future.

What is grief? It is the process of death, gestation, and rebirth. And *all* grief is in some sense *anticipatory* grief. For grief is not a healthy human response to death merely because it allows the individual to overcome negative symptoms. It does not occur to return one from sorrow, anxiety, meaninglessness, hate, and guilt only to the banal. Grief is healthy because it allows the individual to gestate and be reborn. It occurs to move one from the old and banal to new life. Grief is the anticipation of life as well as of death. Those who are able to say only No to death and No to life anticipate nothing. They are the dead in life. But those who say Yes to both death and life by passing through initiatory grief anticipate everything.

The second clue concerns the timing of grief. Primitive man did see death as certain. When this perception is genuine, the time for grief is always "Now." It is always now that man is to die, gestate, and be reborn. Religion is what transforms man's covert and chronic grief into grief that is overt and occasional. Initiatory grief is for every man in every condition.

Consider the puberty rite. Undoubtedly it had something to do with the stage of adolescence. But it was not conceived by the primitives primarily as a tool for fostering maturity. The latter is modern interpretation. Lying in a grave is not the same as reclining on a psychoanalyst's couch. The puberty rite existed to create a human being. Before the rite took place, the boy was not human. He was only an animal which might someday become a human being. A student artist once created a sculpture of a woman in grief. To the surprise of the artist, the pose of the woman was that of the ready-to-be-born, a fetal position. Actually a primitive tale makes the identical point. History began, so the story goes, when all the people were required to pass through a narrow gate and to touch the corpse of a goddess on the other side. Those who passed through the gate and touched "death" became what are now known as human beings. Those who refused and did not touch "death" became what are known as animals and vegetables. The puberty rite and this tale suggest that initiatory grief is for every man.

The time for grief is always the present. It has been said that "man, when he does not grieve, almost ceases to exist." Primitive man understood the situation differently. Man, when he does not grieve—has not begun to exist.

The conclusions of this exercise are: the task of the bereaved is to accept death and accept life; the task is to die, gestate, and be reborn, and the outcome is humanity; and the task is for every man. What is a "finely-finished death"? It is a *death*, not a fading away. Die now or fade later. It is also an uncommon death. A "finely-finished death"—who cares? Most of all a "finely-finished death" is a rebirth.

All the following questions are given to facilitate your participation in anticipatory grief. The first seven assume that our death is distant and certain. They suggest matters to be attended to now for the sake of practical as well as spiritual convenience and well-being. The last three questions assume that our death is near and certain. Physically, this may be so. Spiritually, it should be so.

1. Do you have a will?   Yes____ No____
2. Do you have life insurance?   Yes____ No____
3. Are you willing to have an autopsy done on your body?
                                                          Yes____ No____
4. Are you willing to donate the organs of your body for use after you die?   Yes____ No____

5. How do you want your body disposed of?

Burial	____
Cremation	____
Donated to medical school	____
I do not care	____

6. What kind of last rites do you desire?

Funeral with open casket	____
Funeral with closed casket	____
Funeral with no body present	____
Memorial service	____
I do not care	____

7. Indicate your reaction to the "Living Will" distributed by the Euthanasia Education Council by either signing it or not. Rewrite it as much as you desire.

To MY FAMILY, MY PHYSICIAN, MY CLERGYMAN, MY LAWYER

If the time comes when I can no longer take part in decisions for my own future, let this statement stand as the testament of my wishes:

If there is no reasonable expectation of my recovery from physical or mental disability, I, _____, request that I be allowed to die and not be kept alive by artificial means or heroic measures. Death is as much a reality as birth, growth, maturity and old age—it is the one certainty. I do not fear death as much as I fear the indignity of deterioration, dependence and hopeless pain. I ask that drugs be mercifully administered to me for terminal suffering even if they hasten the moment of death.

This request is made after careful consideration. Although this document is not legally binding, you who care for me will, I hope, feel morally bound to follow its mandate. I recognize that it places a heavy burden of responsibility upon you, and it is with the intention of

sharing that responsibility and of mitigating any feelings
of guilt that this statement is made.

Signed _____

8. You have just been told that you have only 24 hours to
live. What is your *one* greatest *regret* about your life? Be
brief; write only a *few* words. Be *concrete*.

9. You have just been told that you have only 24 hours to
live. What is the *one* thing that you are most *grateful* for
about your life? Be brief; write only a *few* words.

10. For which of the last two questions was it most difficult
to find an answer? Why?

Question 8	___
Question 9	___
Equally difficult	___

REBIRTH

Life in Death

How can a man be born again? First he must die. But then what? Too many die only to remain dead in life. How can the transition be made from death to life? The movement occurs when the two are connected. The function of beliefs about death and the afterlife is to make this connection between life and death. Is there immortality of the soul, resurrection of the body, or is death the absolute end? What are the meanings and implications of such beliefs? And some might query, "Why even bother discussing these beliefs?" They may derive from very orthodox or very unorthodox persuasions.

Answers to these questions are unlikely to be convincing except to those who give them. Yet they are all attempts to connect the fact of life with the fact of death. Thornton Wilder expresses his faith in *Our Town:*

I don't care what they say with their mouths—everybody knows that *something* is eternal. And it ain't houses and it ain't names, and it ain't earth, and it ain't even stars—everybody knows in their bones that *something* is eternal, and *that* something has to do with human beings. All the greatest people ever lived have been telling us that for five thousand years and yet you'd be surprised how people are always losing hold of it. There's something way down deep that's eternal about every human being.[1]

Despite the vagueness, this credo provides meaning for living by asserting that death grants eternity to "something." But the hold on this conviction has been lost. More and more we are crying out like the hero on the last page of one of André Malraux's novels:

You know what they say: "It takes nine months to create a man, and only a single day to destroy him." We both of us have known the truth of this as well as any one could ever know it. . . . Listen, May: it does not take nine months to make a man, it takes fifty years—fifty years of sacrifice, of determination, of—so many things! And when that man has been achieved, when there is no childishness left in him, nor any adolescence, when he is truly, utterly, a man—the only thing he is good for is to die.[2]

This is a bitter expression of the futility of life from a truly, utterly *modern* man, one who has left behind so-called childish beliefs in immortality and resurrection. There is no connection between life and death is this credo. Each one of us probably has some understanding of him because we are partly like him. With respect to the proclamations of tradition, we do not hear so well. The counterproclamation is that we have "come of age." Have we? Can we? Should we? How can death and life be connected in our time?

Before looking at beliefs, this exercise will consider what lies behind them in the experience of the race and of the individual. There are images that come from the childhood of the race and concepts from the childhood of the individual. Neither one nor both together are *the* source or sources of our beliefs, but they are partial causes that illuminate our condition. So we shall examine very primitive images of death, the child's conceptions of death, and then turn to discussion of beliefs in the afterlife. The central issue to be developed concerns the extent to which our beliefs connect life and death.

Images of Death

To consider images of death is to look at what is usually hidden by sophisticated concepts and doctrinal formulations. Although we can determine the images that lie underneath theological treatises by careful analysis it is useful to begin with a more visual approach. We could turn to the literary arts or to the visual arts themselves. But we will look at the images of primitive man, for this has the additional advantage of moving us to other cultures and beyond our preconceptions.[3]

It may be that death has always had an image to human beings. If not, primitive man would have experienced total chaos and responded with total horror. And this would be blind and absolute precisely because there is no image. An image pins death down to some *thing* that can be differentiated from other things. With an image, it can be said that "this thing is horrible and that other thing is not." Living without an image would tend to make the totality of existence horrible. All man could do would be to flee. There is a group of nomadic people in northeast India so primitive that they do not have domestic animals, not even dogs. When a member of the tribe dies, the rest simply run away in panic, never to return if it can be avoided. This is not typical however, since images of death abound among most primitive peoples. Because of them, something more than flight is possible.

Death may be seen as a *corpse* or as a group of corpses. The pictures are of a body in which breathing does not occur and blood does not flow, a body which is decomposing, a skeleton, a ghost. Death is pinned down by images. Consequently, man can do more than flee. He can dispose of the corpse. Fear remains, but it is confined to corpses, burial grounds, and nighttime.

Death may also be seen as the *devourer*. In stumbling upon an abandoned corpse, it appears as though the earth were swallowing it up. The image is of jaws. Earth is like a beast of prey. It is a huge carnivore which will suddenly open its jaws to tear apart and devour the living. The tearing away at flesh and bones by earth's emissaries—dogs, wolves, and hyenas—increases the vividness of the image. Concerning the Greek hound of hell, it was said: "Cerberus is the earth and devours all living things." Primitive man has this perception. Fear of death remains, but burial of the corpse or throwing it to the dogs becomes meaningful behavior.

It may be speculated that the negativism and minimal connection between death and life revealed in these images is overcome when death is viewed anthropomorphically. The inescapability of death becomes justified when death is perceived as *mother* and *father*.

Primitive man saw earth as mother, that which created and sustained him. But if earth is also the jaws of death, then death is mother. Earth is the womb of the mother and the jaws of the wolf. The womb and the jaws are put together in a single image and death is seen as the fertile and yet fatal mother. What creates also devours. By this image, the fundamental opposites of human experience are brought together. The most familiar and the most unfamiliar—life and death—become connected. There is a possibility of something more than flight or passive acceptance. Birth and death have the same source, and moreover, one can be interpreted in terms of the other. Death can bring birth.

The image of death as father is linked to images of corpses and ghosts—the dead. These are to be feared. They are inclined to hang around a village causing destruction and death until final rites are held. At that time, the souls take up their new abode with the community of ancestors. This group of long-deceased fathers possesses great wisdom which the living need. Man often consults them over their graves for advice on important matters. The fathers remain death-dealing butchers who carry off the living. But they possess wisdom which they are to some extent willing to share with those heroic human beings who dare confront them and humbly request it. Of course the heroes must be suitably armed with magical defenses, for the fathers cannot be trusted. And with luck, the hero may even outwit the dead and obtain more wisdom than the fathers desire. By this image of death as father, wisdom and death become related. Again there is a possibility of something more than flight or passive acceptance. Wisdom and death have the same source, and one can be interpreted in terms of the other. Death can bring wisdom.

When images of death as both mother and father exist together in a culture, the full form of death and rebirth is visible. A shaman can travel up the cosmic pillar to the heavens where the fathers instruct him in the mysterious wisdom of life and death, and he can then travel down the cosmic pillar into the bowels of the earth for restoration to life by the mother. So, in India, there are still tales of both the Hindu rope trick and the Hindu basket trick. The coil of rope is thrown into the air and remains suspended, pointing toward the heavenly fathers. The boy or man climbs the rope and disappears. But in the course of receiving wisdom, his body is dismembered. From that invisible realm above the sky, the parts of the body fall to the ground. They are placed in a large basket (mother earth) and covered. Lo and behold, the body is reunited and the person springs out of the basket alive! These two tricks, still performed by stage magicians, have come down from primitive rites of initiation. The rites themselves have come from the even more primitive images of death as mother and father. And these fruitful images could not have sprung into man's consciousness without the prior images of death as the dead and as the devourer.

Such images once enabled man to do more than attempt flight from the inescapable. Images picture similarities as well as distinctions. Because of these connections, primitive man was able to find meaning in death and allow it to affect his life. He died in rites of initiation and received the gifts of rebirth and wisdom.

At the end of this exercise, the same images will be interpreted and applied to our contemporary situation (to do so now would be premature). Appropriate now is the discovery of our own image of death. It could be a corpse, skeleton, ghost, jaws of earth, jaws of an animal, a mother who destroys and nourishes, or a father who destroys and gives wisdom. It could be a gun, tombstone, cross, abstract design, or blackness. It could be almost anything imaginable. The best way to discover it for yourself is to take a sheet of paper and a pen, pencil, or magic marker, and then actually draw an image. Do this now, spending no more than five minutes at the exercise. The purpose is neither demonstration of artistic ability nor depiction of official beliefs. Therefore no drawing can be good or bad, right or wrong. The purpose is the discovery of your own image of death. Do it now, and perhaps you will be surprised by the process and the results. If you do it many times over a period of years, you will make further discoveries as the images that appear develop and change. And if you do this exercise with a small group of people, you can all play the kindergarten game of "show and tell." Sharing of the images and comments on them will highlight the uniqueness of your own image of death. Be assured that actually drawing your image is quite different from just thinking about it.

Concepts of Death

Between our images of death and our beliefs about it lie fundamental concepts. These are the result of many factors, one of which is our conception of death when we were children. Maria Nagy collected data from 378 children living in Budapest in 1948 and organized it according to the dynamics revealed in three developmental stages.[4] Her findings parallel those of other researchers. This review of the content and style of our own early thought provides a clear example of how the child is mother and father of the adult.

Stage one includes children from three through six years of age. In this first stage the child does not know death as such. He attributes life and consciousness to the dead. According to Nagy, there are two steps in this stage. In the first, death is seen as *departure* and *sleep.* A child of four years says: "It can't move because it's in the coffin. . . . It can eat and drink." Another of the same age asserts: "A dead person is just as if he were asleep. . . . A dead person only knows if somebody goes out to the grave or something." The dead can move, eat, and breathe and they can feel and think. They are alive, but in a limited way. Nagy concludes that death is conceived as a departure in which the dead are only somewhat changed. In the second step of this stage, physical death is acknowledged but considered to be a *gradual* or *temporary* event. A child of six asserts: "If he is dead he feels a tiny little bit. When he is quite dead he no longer feels anything." Another child of the same age: "He can't speak. He can't move. Can't see. He lies for four days." Why for only four days? "Because the angels dig him out, take him with them. . . . Only the coffin stays down there." And what happens to the corpse? "If it's a woman, she does the cleaning. If it's a man, then he'll be an angel." Nagy concludes that these children do not know death. The conception of death as departure and sleep is total denial of death. The conceptions of death as gradual or temporary are of an higher order, but still do not fully separate death from life.

Stage two includes children from five through nine years of age. In this stage, death is personified. Death is seen as a separate *person* or as *the dead.* Two thirds of the children conceive of death as a person. A child of seven reports: "What is death? A ghost. . . . Somebody invisible. An invisible man. . . . Comes in the air." The other third in this age group define death as the dead, even though the two terms are quite different in Hungarian. A child of eight says: "Death can't talk because it isn't alive. Death has no mind." The researcher concludes that death is accepted as final and clearly distinct from life. But it is not perceived as universal and inevitable. Those who equate death and the dead show no understanding of death as inevitable for all living creatures. It is just an event which occurs now and then. Those children who perceive a death-man believe that death occurs only to those who are caught and carried off. It is possible to hide or fool death and escape it. One boy had a fantasy about hitting death on the head. Perhaps he had seen the old Punch and Judy puppet show in which Punch does hit Death on the head with his stick and kills him. In this second stage, death is final and frightening, but it is not universal.

The final stage includes children aged nine and above. Death is seen as a process which occurs inevitably according to universal laws. It is not the result of an outer attack, but of an inner process. A child of nine states: "Death is the termination of life. Death is destiny." Another of the same age reports: "If somebody dies they bury him and he crumbles to dust in the earth. . . . Death is something that no one can escape." And another concludes: "What is death? Well, I think it is a part of a person's life. Like school." Nagy concludes that only in this final stage of conceptual development is death seen as distinct from life, final, and universal. In the first stage there is only denial of death. In the second there is fearful recognition with responses of flight and fight. But in the third stage there is acceptance of death as natural.

The following discussion of beliefs considers the implications of these concepts of death in the child. Our immediate task is to become further aware of our own fundamental concepts. It is likely that we are influenced by more than one concept from our childhood, so rank any three of the following, the first being the leading concept in your thinking.

Death as departure   ——
Death as sleep   ——
Death as gradual   ——
Death as temporary   ——
Death as a person   ——
Death as the dead   ——
Death as the inevitable and the universal end   ——

Now compare and contrast the results of your ranking of concepts with your own drawing of an image of death. And consider the fears and hopes that may be related to the concepts you have selected as your own. To what extent has the thought of your own childhood been mother and father of your adulthood?

Beliefs about Death

A world survey of beliefs concerning death and the afterlife would be a gigantic task. A more limited survey of those beliefs held throughout the history of the Western world would be vast in scope. Even a thorough Christian scholar would have to begin with consideration of the variety of beliefs manifest around the Mediterranean during biblical times. And a very narrowly conceived Judaic-Christian study would include the following: (1) early Greek belief in immortality as the communities' memory of the heroic dead; (2) later Greek belief in the soul as preexistent and immortal by nature; (3) early Hebraic belief in Sheol with a stress on corporate personality and survival through the People; (4) later Hebraic apocalyptic belief in resurrection of the dead in the context of a restored People; (5) the variety of views in the New Testament, including the apocalyptic belief of Jesus, the belief of Paul of being asleep until a final resurrection of the body with the dawning of the new order, and the focus of John on rebirth and the quality of present life; (6) the variety of treatments on the themes of immortality and resurrection from the time of the early Church Fathers to the present. Thorough discussion of all these themes would include analysis of the amalgamation of and tension between the beliefs in immortality of the soul and resurrection of the body. Clearly the subject of beliefs in the afterlife, even from such a narrow perspective, is very large.[5]

This section of the exercise is not a theological examination of all these beliefs. It does not discuss ultimate truth. Rather it focuses only on the advantages and disadvantages of beliefs in the afterlife and in death as the end of life. It concludes with a psychological perspective for discovering a belief which both participates in the spirit of the tradition and is functional for contemporary man. Such a belief would connect death and life. Since we are in danger of either ignoring death or worshipping it, and tend to follow alternatively either a God of life or a God of death, our goal is discovery of the God of both life and death.

To perceive the advantage of such beliefs as immortality and resurrection, consider this psychoanalytic commonplace: the stages of childhood development are not left behind, but continue to exist dynamically in the adult. All the conceptions of death in the child are functioning to some degree in the adult as well. There will be variation between adults and within an individual during the course of his adult life, but all these conceptions probably play some role in the attitude of the adult toward death. It follows that an unconscious concept may play a more important role in our reactions to death than the concept of which we are most aware. And what is true of the concepts of childhood is probably also true of the images of the childhood of the race. The dreams of some people do reveal such images as that of death as a wolf. Not only the concepts remain, but also the very concrete and literal style of thinking of the child and the primitive. Recall the incident of the young nurse who had none of the nine fears of death listed on the questionnaire, but was afraid of being buried alive. Perhaps it is not sufficient to claim that her unconscious was playing devious tricks on her in an attempt to cope with her anxiety about death. This highly sophisticated, highly intellectual, psychological point of view may miss the point. The list of fears is a list of abstractions. It would appeal to a person who generalizes and organizes. But her response is very concrete, reminding us of both primitives and children. She may be defining death itself as being buried alive. Who was in flight from fear—the nurse or the composer of the questionnaire?

These images and beliefs serve as preconditions for beliefs about death. In the first stage of the childhood concepts, death as departure is a precondition for the belief in immortality of the soul, and death as temporary is a precondition for belief in resurrection. Note that a devaluation of the body may not be necessary for the former belief to occur, nor acquaintance with the planting of seeds and harvest of grain be necessary for appearance of the latter. Such things would be important cultural preconditions which are added to the individual developmental ones. The personification of death in stage two is a precondition for the more sophisticated images of death as a person in the myths, legends, and fairy tales of our culture. The concept of universal dissolution of the body is not the same as, but is the precondition for, the scientific belief that the death of the body is a death of the total personality. Belief behavior is *over*determined, but two of the causes for beliefs about the afterlife are the variety of images and concepts stemming from the development of the individual and of mankind. Believers function *consciously* as primitives and children do, while nonbelievers tend to function *unconsciously* as primitives and children do. To be a believer is to be in touch with a fundamental aspect of the inner reality of the psyche.

Another advantage for those who believe in immortality of the soul or resurrection of the body is that they are put in touch with the outer reality of death itself. The point would be disputed by many contemporary thinkers who suspect or claim that such beliefs function as tools for denial. But "denial" is a term used all too casually.

In the report on children's concepts, Nagy concluded that the first stage of death as departure and sleep is a stage of denial. At the very least, this is misleading. Denial is usually understood as a way of getting rid of unwelcome facts by claiming that they do not exist. It is assumed that one who denies is one who sees what is the case and then runs from it, or is capable of seeing what is the case but refuses to do so. What is perceived or capable of being perceived is a threat to the existence of the ego. Denial is a protection against this threat. The question arises: is this dynamic the source of the four-year-old's concept of death as departure or as temporary? There is certainly some room for doubt. The young child may not be capable of perceiving the unwelcome "fact" adults call death. And what he cannot grasp intellectually he has no need to deny emotionally. Further, it is obvious that this supposed "denial" does not function well as a defense. The basic threat to the child *is* the mother's departure, whether as a corpse or in some other form of travel. So if the child's concept did serve the function of denial, it would be the least effective of all such protective maneuvers. Each stage in the child's development is neutral from the standpoint of mental health and undoubtedly has its own cluster of fears and defenses against them.

This same understanding should be applied to adults. It is common for modern man to proclaim that beliefs in life after death are mechanisms of denial of reality. The issue is more complicated. Denial certainly operates in this area, but only in part. An adult whose approach to death is basically ruled by a concept from the first stage may not be denying, but simply responding to what he is most capable of seeing as "reality." Religious beliefs and rituals are, at the very least, methods of coping with perceived reality. They may involve more or less recognition of death. And it is an even chance that they allow as much recognition of death as is allowed by the absence of belief. What allows man to cope may be abused, but without it, man simply flees. Unless there is strong proof to the contrary, it should not be assumed that beliefs in the afterlife are necessarily mechanisms of denial. Such beliefs are basic tools for enabling man to perceive and respond to the issues of his life and death.

Those who believe in immortality of the soul or resurrection of the body have the advantages of being put in touch with both the inner reality of the psyche and the outer reality of death. But there are also serious disadvantages. We live in an age of demythologization and remythologization. The beliefs in immortality and resurrection are formulated in ways that do not fit our understanding. The old three-story universe has been replaced by a one-storied or infinitely storied universe, depending on how you prefer to state it. Familiar understandings of heaven and hell and purgatory (although certainly not familiar to Jesus and Paul) do not fit our view of the universe. It could be argued that the location of the afterlife is not important. But it is curious that our declining religious interest in the location of heaven and hell is matched by declining understanding of the nature and function of space. This dimension is the "hidden dimension" for modern man. It might be wiser for believers to locate heaven and hell on distant stars in this or another galaxy, or place them in antiworlds, rather than either to cling to old formulations or abandon the theme of location. Our focus on time, kinds of time, and myths has been to the detriment of our understanding of space, kinds of space, and ritual. In the povery of our appreciation of space and with the collapse of traditional views, the traditional beliefs are neither appropriate to our age nor functional for the individual. If this is the case, then holding to the beliefs as traditionally understood is a disservice to the gospel.

The two conscious beliefs most prevalent in our time are the scientific belief that death is the end of the personality and the popular religious belief that the personality or soul survives death. It is obvious enough that most of us are partially ruled by the concept of the third stage—inevitable dissolution of the body—and so open to the belief that death is the end. But it is interesting that this concept and belief is matched by the concept and belief arising from the earliest part of the first stage. The vast majority, nearly 100 percent of Protestant church people, believe in immortality. And what naturally accompanies this is the fear of separation from loved ones. The popular meaning of immortality is reunion with loved ones. With the concept of dissolution of the body, we might expect to meet fear of the pain of dying and fear of extinction; with the concept of death as a person, we might expect to meet fear of violence and punishment; but what we do meet is fear of departure—anxiety over travel. What we face in ourselves most commonly as contemporary adults are the two poles of the developmental path.

If this is the case concerning our conscious life, then two problems occur. First of all, these beliefs are at war with each other. On the one hand, death is believed to be totally distinct from life, final and inevitable. On the other hand, death is believed to be not so distinct from life and not final at all. The two beliefs are completely opposed. Secondly, both beliefs seem to require no effort, struggle, or discipline for the believer. With respect to the child, neither concept makes any demands on him. Either the body lives on and that is that, or the body disintegrates and that is that. The adult beliefs entail the same lack of demand. If death is the absolute end, there is nothing one can do about it. If death is not the end and there is immortality, then according to popular religion there is nothing one need do about this. It just occurs. What we have in modern man are two beliefs which are not only opposed but irreconcilable. If, for example, immortality depended on human behavior or upon God's behavior, then the beliefs could be reconciled: death would be the end, unless man or God intervened. But this is not the situation. Both beliefs refer to automatic processes about which nothing can be done. So with respect to conscious beliefs, modern man is experiencing a serious conflict.

However, there is a largely unconscious belief which needs to be explored. Between the first and third developmental stages lies the stage of personification of death. For the child at this age, death is a cruel and violent person who can snatch him away from life. But the death-man can be avoided and even fought. Death is final but not inevitable. This appears to be the only concept of death in the child which allows human struggle with death to occur. The beliefs which would follow from the concept do not appear at all frequently in modern man's consciousness. Little evidence has been collected to demonstrate its rule in the unconscious. But underneath our matter-of-fact beliefs in death as the end and death as followed by immortality may lie belief in death as a violent butcher who can and must be battled. Here death would be aggressive, accidental, and avoidable. After indicating his preference as to knowing the time and mode of his own death, one person asked why the place of death was not included. When asked why he wanted to know it, he responded: "So I could be somewhere else!" And death is sexual and fascinating as well. It is a rapist or seducer. In a statement on one's own death, an individual wrote:

Death calls up for me deep bodily reactions—I see a lonely beach with huge waves, refuse on the beach, bodies of fish and serpents, rocks, shells, all refuse of death, and the waves pounding on the shore constantly, not quite rhythmically, unceasing. The waves hit the rocks and the spray disappears into the air. The sea is hypnotic and very fearful. The waves are huge and inviting and forbidding. I wade into the edge and the waves pound me down; I get to my feet and it pounds me down again. The pounding waves are tremendously exciting, deeply sexually exciting, thrilling, exhilarating, but it alternates with fear and terror, being swept off my feet and thrown against the rocks and sand on the beach, smothered and drowned by the relentless waves. I gasp for breath in excitement and fear. . . .

The suspicion that we personify death is borne out by two small research studies.[6] In one, a group of college students were asked to rank the following metaphors in terms of their appropriateness in describing death: an understanding doctor, a gay seducer, a grinning butcher, a last adventure, a threatening father, a misty abyss, the end of a song. The women tended to pick "a gay seducer" as most appropriate; the men tended to pick "a grinning butcher." Most of the metaphors are personifications, but note the two themes which predominated: *sex and aggression*. Another piece of research consisted of collecting fantasies from women who were dying of cancer and comparing them with those of similar women hospitalized for minor illnesses. This was followed by a second study of women with other types of fatal illnesses. In both cases most of the fatally ill knew that they were dying. The results clearly indicated that fatally ill women fantasied largely about sex and aggression. The themes were illicit sex and punishment. More specifically, the theme is of a mysterious stranger who traps the woman into sexual intercourse against her will with the result of pleasure, guilt, and punishment. It is concluded that for many dying women, death is conceptualized as an evil seducer. Unfortunately, no known research seeks to discover how much men conceptualize death as a witch—a beautiful, enticing woman who beguiles man to his death.

One must conclude, first, that we ought to look for this personification of death in ourselves, for it may have more bearing on our behavior toward death than our conscious beliefs. Second, exploration of the belief would serve to break up the conflict between beliefs in automatic death and automatic immortality. And third, this primitive and childlike personification of death possesses a dynamic view which is at least similar to the more advanced belief of traditional Christianity. In their own ways, both conceive of death as related to sin and judgment and both conceive of death as final and universal unless battled and overcome. Life and death are connected in a vital way.

Beliefs in immortality and resurrection are significant because they have the advantages of tapping the primitive images and childlike conceptions of the psyche, but they may border on insignificance due to the changed perception of the universe and the clash of known and unknown beliefs in a pluralistic society. They may no longer connect death and life. A belief that death spells the absolute end of human life begins to appear attractive in view of the alternatives traditionally provided.

The advantages of the belief that death is annihilation are quite apparent to our age. We can see that this is so and remember and anticipate that it should be so. This has been true for men of all ages. The knowledge that the dead are dead is affirmed, however indirectly, throughout history. However, this perception has always been one of several, whereas it is coming to be our one and only perception. The outer empiricism of our time in philosophy and science tends to rule so that death is conceived ideologically as a natural process of dissolution. This belief has the advantage of fitting into our perception of existence. It is a relief to dismiss those beliefs that have been passed on from people with different world views. It means an end to conflict over opposed beliefs. And it means an end to theological doubletalk about these beliefs. Most important, the belief that death is the end can lead to a greater awareness of the significance of human relationships, to a new appreciation of love and community. This is the claim of some and the hope of many.

In this age of realism, we should ask just how realistic this hope is. According to Albert Camus, existence is absurd and one cannot escape from absurdity by suicide or belief in another life. At the end of *The Stranger*, a chaplain guesses that Meursault must have wished that there were an afterlife. Meursault responds:

Of course I had, I told him. Everybody has that wish at times. But that had no more importance than wishing to be rich, or to swim very fast, or to have a better-shaped mouth. It was in the same order of things. I was going on in the same vein, when he cut in with a question. How did I picture the life after the grave?

I fairly bawled out at him: "A life in which I can remember this life on earth. That's all I want of it." And in the same breath I told him I'd had enough of his company.[7]

We should note that this expression is offered by a condemned man, one who is fully aware of his forthcoming death. Camus offers a this-wordly view that is fully aware of the deaths of individuals and groups. In *The Plague* one of the heroes says: "The order of the world is shaped by death." Here is realism. The setting of this work is death, a bubonic plague, and it is intended to depict the present experience of our culture. But the theme is love and community. After the plague is over, the narrator ruminates:

As to what that exile and that longing for reunion meant, Rieux had no idea . . . he was thinking it has no importance whether such things have or have not a meaning; all we need consider is the answer given to men's hope.

They knew now that if there is one thing one can always yearn for, and sometimes attain, it is human love.

If others . . . had got what they wanted, this was because they had asked for the one thing that depended on them solely. And . . . Rieux was thinking it was only right that those whose desires are limited to man and his humble yet formidable love, should enter, if only now and again, into their reward.

. . . Dr. Rieux resolved to compile this chronicle, so that he should not be one of those who hold their peace but should bear witness in favor of those plague-stricken people; so that some memorial of the injustice and outrage done them might endure; and to state quite simply what we learn in a time of pestilence: that there are more things to admire in men than to despise.

None the less, he knew that the tale he had to tell could not be one of a final victory. It could be only the record of what had had to be done, and what assuredly would have to be done again in the never-ending fight against terror and its relentless onslaughts, despite their personal afflictions, by all who, while unable to be saints but refusing to bow down to pestilences, strive their utmost to be healers.[8]

The novel is a chronicle of *heroism.* Its theme is a very modest one: in the face of suffering and death, we are to *endure, love,* and *heal.* For Camus, there is meaning in this and there is no meaning greater than this. In a crisis of life and death, men may meet each other. This is the hope and this is the ultimate reward.

I first read *The Plague* because it was recommended by a man in his early thirties who was dying from a lengthy and debilitating disease. He said that it stated his own understanding far better than he could himself. I read it, was overwhelmed, and remain so. Death does prompt us to hold one another and, thus, to heal one another. Life and death are connected by love. This is a clear advantage of the belief that death is the end.

In his discussion of Camus, Milton McC. Gatch concludes that the author is an ideal example of modern awareness, specifically awareness of *isolation* between men and between communities. Gatch observes:

Life is purposive in that the community of men finds ways to cope with the absurd; but life is isolated in that there is no continuum within which the community of men can formulate the universal or historical significance of their experience in the face of death.[9]

This observation, together with thorough examination of Christian tradition concerning immortality and resurrection, prompts Gatch to state a somewhat different view of death as the end. After careful discussion of traditional beliefs, Gatch concludes that Christian tradition focuses more on life than on death and that the meaning of death is to be found in life. The Christian urgency is not about death, but about life. Therefore he argues, what needs to be preserved is the "tone" of traditional teaching rather than its form or content. Both beliefs are to be replaced by the belief that death is the end of the individual. What is to be retained is the traditional Christian concern for the mundane life, historical awareness, and the sense of urgency about our actions with regard to the future. Immortality and resurrection are perceived as modes rather than facts:

> The issue is whether man should be and can be more interested in his subjective existence or in his social existence. The mode of resurrection calls upon man to live hard and well and boldly here and now and to understand that what he does is important in the historical continuum. The mode of immortality calls upon man to concern himself above all with his inner or mental or spiritual development and to regard his place in history as of secondary concern.[10]

The author believes that both elements are essential, but lays his emphasis quite clearly on the side of the mode of resurrection—the struggle of society to fulfill the promise of a vision of a new world. By means of this focus, Gatch attempts to maintain and expand the concerns of Camus, adding the hope for understanding of the universal or historical significance of our responses to life and death. His purpose is to maintain our current involvement with concrete realities of life and add historical perspective and historical hope. Life and death are connected by community.

The aspirations of Camus and Gatch involve disadvantages. Concerning the approach of Camus, it may be said that the ego-chill we experience in the face of death does not always lead to more profound relationship with others. Our reaction at times is quite the reverse: withdrawal. Furthermore, when the chill lessens, our outreach frequently lessens. Crises of death come and go. To some extent our humanity appears to come and go with them.

The conclusion of Gatch is an attempt to mediate between the insights of the Christian tradition and the perceptions and needs of contemporary man. It is important to note that he has worked through the tradition rather than bypassed it. The result is a "secular" understanding which does preserve the spirit of the tradition. It may preserve more than this, more even than the author acknowledges himself. He retains the terms "immortality" and "resurrection" although giving them a new interpretation. Such terms give rise to a host of intellectual and emotional associations which support the interpretation—consciously and unconsciously. These are associations with the Christian beliefs. If the terms were entirely eliminated, the powerful support of the tradition would diminish. And awareness of universal and historical perspectives would diminish. The terms also become linked to the images and concepts discussed previously. These fundamental and organizing creations enable man to perceive death as a reality. Such linkage is mostly an unconscious activity. So Gatch may be relying on a great many images and concepts and traditions which support and render his final stance *functional*.

The suggestion is that the nature of man and the nature of our history indicate that human beings must deal quite directly with their awareness of death, just as directly as they must deal with life. Certainly we find the meaning of death in our lives, but we also find the meaning of life in our deaths. Connecting life and death involves more than proclaiming the value of community. Our battle for the future of mankind must take fully into account our primitive and childlike responses to death. Otherwise, our preoccupation with community and justice will become that flight from death which leads to self-destruction. Beliefs that death is the end and that the goal for man is to transform the world may be the most functional beliefs for contemporary man. But they have a subjective aspect as well as the obvious social one. We must consider the subjective as carefully as the social, if only for the reason of preventing the subjective from overturning and ruling the social.

For the remainder of this exercise, we consider possibilities for our own growth in belief. Modern man has not come of age. Rather we are between childhood and adulthood—in the time of adolescence. With regard to death, we hang on to the old beliefs of immortality and resurrection at times; we hang on to the new belief of death as the end at other times; we hold on to all at the same time, and we are hung by them. The hanging will have to continue for a while. The danger lies in quitting this stage through precipitous flight from either old beliefs or the new one. What is required is more creative meeting between the primitive images and concepts and the modern perspective.

The thesis of these exercises is that grief is implicitly initiatory and anticipatory of new life. The profound crisis of death raises the hope of beginning life over again. And this hope uncovers our childhood concepts and primitive images. Grief becomes explicitly anticipatory when these concepts and images arise to connect our experiences of death and life. Grief drives man to initiatory death and rebirth. Camus and Gatch understand that the prospect of physical death creates a sense of urgency about the quality of one's life. What needs to be understood as well is that the physical demand that we must die gives rise to the demand that we must die spiritually. Without this realization, the call for love and community is liable to be little more than a momentary desperate sentimentality.

We might try standing with humility before our own childhood concepts of death. Recall the statement of the hero in Malraux's novel. It is true that it takes fifty years to make an adult and that all that is left is to die. But the author's mood of futility may be related to an overevaluation of adult concepts of death. We are always tempted to overvalue the end of any developmental process; or, in revolt, to overvalue the beginning of the process. Preparation for death is the task of the last half of life and this task involves a return to so-called "childishness." The concepts of death of the child are all still within us to some degree. The task is to bring them into consciousness. Perhaps the path to follow would be the original path of the child in reverse: begin where we are with death as inevitable dissolution of the body; then explore death as the dead and death as a person; and then death as temporary and as departure. But this would be only half of the path. Otherwise there would be overvaluation of the beginning of the developmental process. The second half of the path would be a return to the third stage. At this point, our belief that death is the end would remain, but considerably transformed by additional understanding. Or perhaps this path is circular and unending. No one stage on this path is to be valued more than another. In the adult as in the child, each stage and its concept of death can serve the individual. In psychoanalytic jargon, this process is called "regression in service of the ego," and it means not only regression but also progression in service of the ego. Intellectual exploration of our own childhood concepts can help to connect our experiences of death and life.

We might also stand more humbly before our own primitive images of death. Recall that the most primitive humans were without clear images, and their response to death was flight. It is reasonable to guess that the modern individual who sees death as the end in a simplistic way may have the same response. Encountering our own images may well increase our fear, but this could be appropriate. Some of us are like the boy in the fairy tale who knew no fear. He was not terrified by a ghost at midnight nor by confrontation with a hanged man. On finding a dead man in a coffin, he took the corpse to bed with him to warm it. The boy was not human. So he set out on a journey *to learn to shudder.* Certainly one stage in the path for modern man is to expose himself to the horror of death and develop the capacity to shudder. To take this step is to become a human being capable of fear. And as the primitive discovery of death as jaws and as the dead led to the creative images of death as mother and father, so also could our own exploration carry us beyond shuddering into new life. Expressive exploration in art or craft of our own primitive images may help connect our experiences of death and life.

It is likely that our images of death must be ambivalent ones for the theme of death and rebirth to occur. Positive images of death are as destructive as negative ones. When mother and father become totally beneficent, the trials and tribulations of man are no longer necessary. Life and wisdom are simply handed to us on a platter, at least so we think. But what may really happen with the all-good and all-powerful mother and father gods is that they no longer rule as gods of death. Death is given over to some lesser god such as Satan or ignored altogether. When this happens, death is either unrelated to life or not really death at all. Contemplate modern man with his "nice-guy" God and his tendency to see death as unrelated to life or as unreal. Development from ambivalent images of death to more completely positive ones is not a sign of progress. Indeed, it is leading to the opposite image. Our God of life only is being replaced by a God of death only. We pass from denial of death to worship of death and back to denial again. This path is the endless one of death in life for the individual and the society. The one we must meet in our time must be the God of both life and death.

A final possibility for developing our own belief about death and life involves both intellectual and expressive exploration. What man does best in the face of death is to tell a story. A story combines images and concepts, and surpasses both in profundity of feeling and thought. And everyone can tell a story about death, even if they have never told a story before. Most of us find it easy to write a statement about death, answer questionnaires, and draw an image, but assume that we are incapable of telling a story about the same subject. This is not the case. Telling a story about death is just as easy and far more informative. Everyone who actually writes down a short story is surprised that a story does appear. Even more surprising is the content. One person drew the head of a monster with open jaws as his image of death. For his childhood concept, he selected that of death as the universal and inevitable end. Here is his story:

After the Fall, what happened when the first man died from disease? It was one thing for God to demand obedience, proclaim judgment and institute suffering and death. It was quite another for him to witness a dying human being. When it happened, God was struck dumb. No Word. Then God wept. He picked up the man, pressed him to his breast, and cradled him in his arms. And on the Lord God's face there appeared a wistful look that remains to this day.

The story does not contradict the fearful image and the concept of death as the end. But the teller was surprised by the appearance of God and his wistful comfort. There was more to his perception of death and connecting of death and life than he was aware. Similar surprises are in store for you when you tell your story about death. And the story you tell will provide guidelines for further exploration of a path that is uniquely yours. Take fifteen or twenty minutes right now to write your own story about death. The tale you tell is a gift. And if you and others share your stories about death, you will be surprised by one another into a stronger community. In such a community, beliefs about the afterlife will become more meaningful and less necessary.

In the Midst of Death

Before participating in these exercises in dying and living, one individual reflected:

I don't usually think about thinking about death because I usually have things I want to think about more, or at least more than I want to think about death which is not really, at least at this point, something which scares me, but something which is foreign to me, which is to say, of course, that I have never died or even seen people dead, although I have seen lots of small animals that died or were dead or were at least lying very still with their eyes glazed over, which sort of reminds me of a period at the end of a long sentence.

After the exercises are concluded, participants have much more to reflect upon—their own denial, fear, living death, grief, and beliefs. They tend to contemplate dying and living rather than death per se. But the purpose of these exercises is to facilitate more than intellectual development. The goal is to assist movement from death to life. Death can be experienced as something more than a period ending a life sentence. In the midst of death we can be in life. How are we to be reborn?

The theme of this final exercise is love, the kind of love humbly noted in the following report:

I was returning from hunting, and walking along an avenue of the garden, my dog running in front of me.

Suddenly he took shorter steps, and began to steal along as though tracking game.

I looked along the avenue, and saw a young sparrow, with yellow about its beak and down on its head. It had fallen out of the nest . . . and sat unable to move, helplessly flapping its half-grown wings.

My dog was slowly approaching it, when, suddenly darting down from a tree close by, an old dark-throated sparrow fell like a stone right before his nose, and all ruffled up, terrified, with despairing and pitiful cheeps, it flung itself twice towards the open jaws of shining teeth.

It sprang to save; it cast itself before its nestling . . . but all its tiny body was shaking with terror; its note was harsh and strange. Swooning with fear, it offered itself up! What a huge monster must the dog have seemed to it! And yet it could not stay on its high branch out of danger. . . . A force stronger than its will flung it down.

My Tresor stood still, drew back. . . . Clearly he too recognized this force.

I hastened to call off the disconcerted dog, and went away, full of reverence.

Yes: do not laugh. I felt reverence for that tiny heroic bird, for its impulse of love. Love, I thought, is stronger than death or the fear of death. Only by it, by love, life holds together and advances.[1]

It is doubtful that birds experience what human beings call love. And there is a danger of being sentimental about the relation of love and death. It is too easy glibly to mention love as the solution to all problems of dying and death. It is too easy to assert that all the varied forms of denial and fear rule because of absence of love. It is too easy to claim that suicide differs dynamically from martyrdom because it lacks the motivation of love. And it is too easy to proclaim that all the fundamental opposition over beliefs about life after death is dissolved by the criterion of love. Yet love is a solution to all these problems. Love is stronger than death because it moves us through death into gestation and rebirth. Those who are glib about it discover more about themselves than about love. Our consideration of love as martyrdom may prevent such superficiality.

Clear examples of martyrdom in the Western world come

from the period of persecution of the early Christians. Tertullian wrote:

During the zealous persecution of Arrisu Antonius in Asia all the Christians of a city assembled and presented themselves in a body at his tribunal. He ordered a few of them to execution and remarked to the rest, "Unhappy creatures! If you want to die, you can find precipices and halters for yourselves."[2]

Many Christians did just that. A young woman, Perpetua, after being gored in the arena by a bull, took the hand of a gladiator and moved the sword point to her throat. Ignatius, bishop of Antioch, was condemned to fight wild beasts at Rome and feared that some Christians might work to get him pardoned. He wrote to them:

I dread your very love, lest it should do me a wrong. . . . Oh, that I may enjoy the wild beasts that are prepared for me. I will entice them to make short work of me. . . . If they will not do it of their own accord, I will make them do it. Come fire and cross and grapplings with wild beasts, wrenching of bones, hacking of limbs, crushing of my whole body, cruel tortures of the devil, only let me attain to Jesus Christ.[3]

Thousands of people in the Christian tradition have expressed this apparent delight in death. How can we understand what seems so disgusting, dreadful, and demented?

A classic definition of martyrdom is offered by Karl Rahner.[4] He says three things about it. First, he notes that the biblical meaning of "martyrdom" is "witness." A martyr is one who witnesses to his faith. Second, he observes that by the second century the term had become related to death. Since that time a Christian martyr has been defined as one who *witnesses through death*. Third, Rahner proclaims about man: "He should hurry not towards a death which is the consummation of emptiness, a final pouring out of life into senselessness, but towards a death which is the valid consummation of his existence."[5] These three points suggest a definition: Martyrdom is a witness through death which consummates life. We will explore the dynamics of martyrdom by considering first our witnessing through death and then our consummation of life. Our goal is to discover for our own time what Churchill did during the Battle of Britain: that "this was a time when it was equally good to live or die."

Witness Through Death

The most basic thing to note about a martyr is his delight in change. Some of us find the martyr bizarre because we are afraid of change and he represents the most extreme acceptance of it. We want to preserve our identity at all costs. Any novelty or surprise frightens us and we develop all sorts of methods for ignoring or modifying an event so we can maintain ourselves as we are. A strange inner event, such as an odd dream or impulse to do something unusual, makes us anxious and fearful of becoming mentally ill. We wonder if we really are who we think we are. A strange outer event, such as being avoided by a friend, or even being liked by a stranger, gives rise to anxiety. Again, we wonder if we really are who we think we are. We may not like the self we have, but it is all we know. We make the tacit assumption that there can be no new self.

Death is the most striking example of change. Any event in life has an aspect of unknowableness and mystery, but death most of all. So those of us who grieve rather quietly over change all our lives, are precipitated into great grief over the death of a loved one or distress at our own death. We die and face death as we live—with the fear that our self will sustain a loss. When her husband leaves for a long trip, a wife commonly remarks: "Be careful, I wouldn't want anything to happen to you." The remark indicates the way we face both life and death: we do not want anything to happen. A "happening" is interpreted negatively. In one sense, we are right: any happening leads to loss. But what we cannot understand is that any happening provides opportunity for gain. It is no wonder that death frightens us and martyrdom seems bizarre. For the martyr is one who is not anxious about his life and who takes no thought for the morrow. He accepts change with the delight of his witness.

For delight in change occurs in the martyr because he is a witness. The martyr has a *cause*. He lives and dies in order for something to happen—not to prevent a happening. Since life itself, both within and outside of the individual, is flux, movement, process, the martyr is one who is fully alive. Change in the world and change in the self are inseparable. Thus to participate in a cause is to both change the world and change oneself. The martyr knows that any happening means a loss of his world and of himself, but he also knows that it will be gain for the world and himself. He hurries toward death for the sake of change. This is dying and this is living.

The problem is that just any cause will not do. The last words, "Tell mother—tell mother—I died for my country," were spoken by John Wilkes Booth![6] We need to consider criteria for causes which lead to true martyrdom. There are false causes, powerless causes, and hopeless causes.

There can be false causes, leading to false martyrdom. Here the cause is oneself. Death can be chosen for the sake of only oneself and be an attempt to conform the world to one's self-image. We do not possess the type of information needed to pass judgment, but consider the negative possibilities with respect to the early Christians. Such apparent searching for death could have served to maintain the self in many ways. "I am guilty, therefore I must punish myself." "I am guilty, therefore I must provoke others to punish me." "Nobody cares for me, so I will make them pity me." "Nobody knows I'm alive. They don't pay attention, so I will exhibit myself." "I hate them all, so I'll make them feel guilty." These and other motivations can be directed toward the world in an attempt to change it for one's own purposes. Many Christians have probably sought to change the world in order to avoid changing themselves. The physical death is incidental! One's magnificent self rises straight to heaven without change. The false martyr is like most of us sinners in that his witness is to himself, only he is a little more active and desperate about it. True Christians, however many there were, had a cause other than themselves, one that challenged them as well as challenging the world. It is the *comprehensiveness* of such a cause that engenders true martyrdom.

There are also powerless causes which do not lift one up to martyrdom. The problem is that comprehensive causes tend to be abstract. Truth, Love, Justice, Mankind—these are some of the comprehensive causes for which a man could give his life. Perhaps Socrates and a few others have done so. But most of us find it difficult to be motivated by abstractions. So we retreat to lesser causes and participate in a kind of minor martyrdom. The abstractions are reduced to the concrete items of spouse, children, community, or nation. Such entities are sufficiently specific for us to be devoted to them and die for them. Our deaths may be false martyrdoms, for the things we die for are at least partial extensions of ourselves. The point is that the cause needs to be both comprehensive enough to warrant devotion and concrete enough to make it possible. And nothing is more concrete to a human being than another human being. The early Christians had such a comprehensive and concrete cause in Jesus Christ.

Finally, there are hopeless causes which also fail to engender martyrdom. People do not tend to commit themselves to death for a cause they believe to be hopeless. This is just not in the nature of human beings. Those who have died with apparent hopelessness are either deranged or fooling themselves. Whether the goal is personal bravery, eventual justice, or eternal life, martyrdom can occur only with strong hope of success. The martyr believes, not just that victory will occur, but that victory has already occurred. This is quite a boost to one's morale. And how does he know that victory has occurred? Because that comprehensive and concrete cause is a person, or persons, who has undergone martyrdom himself and emerged victorious. It is this hope which creates the gracefulness of true martyrdom. Without it we become fanatics, people motivated by a destructive despair to kill themselves and the world. Knowing that Christ had assured the victory and pointed the way, some early Christians had both the freedom not to force the cause and the grace to assist the cause in their dying. No martyr considers himself "the first martyr."

There are three criteria for the cause which fosters true martyrdom. It must be comprehensive, concrete, and hopeful. This is a tall order. Few such causes appear on the human scene at any given time. For Christians, Christ is such a cause. To have Christ as the cause is to have a comprehensive one which relates not only to the individual, but to his fellow men and even to all of nature. As an incarnation of God, Christ is concrete and highly suitable for human devotion. And as a victorious martyr, he both assures ultimate hope and points the way.

There have been martyrs in many times and places, both before and after the period of persecution of the early Christians. And martyrdom occurs in a variety of situations quite disconnected from religious and political concerns. The profound fulfillment of witness through death is possible for a contemporary person who is terminally ill. That delight in change which occurs through witness to a cause which is comprehensive, concrete, and hopeful can appear in those who discover physical death to be inevitable and significant.

Recall the depictions of deathbed scenes in classical and contemporary art. Traditional paintings of the scene tend to be similar. The last hours of the dying man are shown to include a host of people gathered around his bed—family, relatives, friends, servants, and important people from his village. All the varying emotions of man are present on their faces. The artist focuses our attention on the dying man himself. Frequently the mood of the picture is one of anticipation, for he is about to utter his last words. Or it may be one of quiet joy as he places his hand on the head of a young child and gives a blessing. Whatever the mood, the event is portrayed as being of great significance.

A modern artist, Edvard Munch, pictures a quite different reaction in his "Death in the Sick Chamber." The focus is not on the dying individual. He cannot be seen, and the people are not gathered around his bed but scattered about the room, and they are not looking at him. Moreover, neither are they looking at one another. The living are separated from the dying individual and from each other. More shocking is the expression on their faces. Although the artist has a naturalistic style, the faces are not human. They do not look natural, for there is no expression on them. They are blank. There is no sign of love or hate, hope or despair, joy or sorrow. There is no sign of significance. There is no sign of anything. Nothing is happening.

The differing moods of classic and modern portrayals of the deathbed scene reflect our attitudes about dying. Death is no longer a great occasion. We desire to die quickly and at night, in our sleep. The most common reason given for this reaction is that such a death "would mean less trouble for everyone concerned." Our goal is to die with little fuss. The death of modern man tends to have no significance.

This insignificance is due partially to the absence of self-conscious martyrdom. The possibility of significance has been discovered by a psychiatrist in the course of his work with dying patients.[7] Through trial and error he found that he had to do more than simply help the patient face the fact of this forthcoming death. He had to set up a situation in which he could give the patient a *gift* which would be received as unusual and unmerited. The patient would experience the gift as the physicians's giving up of a part of himself. The psychiatrist discovered that the patient would then see that they were both dying together. And the patient would be right. To give of oneself to the dying is to accompany him in the experience. More than this, the patient's attitude would be transformed from "having to die" to "dying for you." Because of this gift of love, the patient responds with love and finds his own death appropriate and meaningful. The dying patient can die as a martyr when he finds someone for whom he can die.

What the psychiatrist discovered has always been known by religious traditions. But Christian tradition has limited the act of martyrdom to those circumstances in which there is an opportunity to escape physical death. Karl Rahner claims that "it must be a death which could have been avoided in its concrete reality. It must . . . be a death which is caused by external violence and which could have been avoided by the exercise of freedom."[8] This understanding serves as a safeguard against superficial spiritualizing of the act of martyrdom. But outer circumstances are given more than their due. Whether physical death can be avoided or not, the martyr is one who changes "I might die" or "I have to die" into "I am dying for you." This change can occur regardless of outer circumstances and is motivated by a new or revitalized cause.

The challenge for the dying is to discover something or someone to die for. Unfortunately, we are accustomed to be superficially tender, considerate, and polite to them. We do not think it proper to make demands. Instead we give straightforward comfort and assurance. But assurances are not reassuring unless accompanied by demands. The kind of love we often show to the dying is questionable. We tend to pamper them just as we pamper children. Children who are pampered become warped personalities who do not mature. Living and dying, human beings have responsibilities, and our love for those at the point of death must be the kind of love which makes demands on those who receive it. This does not mean that we walk into a dying person's room and crudely require that he immediately "shape up." Such a demand is at the opposite extreme from pampering and just as ineffective. Both extremes are undoubtedly attempts to reassure oneself rather than the dying patient. The task is not to hit a person over the head with an ideal, but

to encourage him to move in the direction of it. Minor martyrdom is better than no martyrdom at all.

Johnny Gunther was seventeen when he died of a brain tumor after an illness of fifteen months. Soon after he was told of
the nature of his illness, he wrote an "Unbeliever's Prayer."

Almighty God forgive my my agnosticism; for I shall try to keep it
gentle, not cynical, nor a bad influence. And O! if Thou art truly in the
heavens, accept my gratitude for all Thy gifts and I shall try to fight
the good fight. Amen.[9]

He was not an orthodox believer, but his response to death was
one of thanksgiving for all that he had received. In his own way,
however limited by traditional standards, he met his responsibility and faced God. And he received and demonstrated the
gift of love. When a surgeon told him that he had a brain tumor,
Johnny's first comment was: "Do my parents know this? How
shall we break it to them?" His immediate concern was not for
himself, but for the ones he loved. And toward the end of his
life, he illustrated what the psychiatrist has discovered and the
Christian tradition has always known. The tumor which was
killing him had raised a large bump on the top of his head. One
day he obscurely and quietly announced: "Perhaps I'm having
the bump for you." His parents were too moved to reply. But
their account of his death reveals how much Johnny did for
them.

The conclusion is that our own dying can be significant regardless of whether or not death can be avoided. We need not
remain tied to the defensive desire for death to occur unbe-
knownst to us during sleep, as an occasion for little fuss. The
natural demand for a physical death is to be matched by a
supernatural demand for a spiritual death. And we cannot just
go ahead and die in order to be granted a new life. We cannot
pull ourselves down into death and up into life again by our own
bootstraps. But we can discover or be discovered by a cause
outside ourselves. To fully discover a cause is to die to oneself

and be reborn, and the following of the cause is a deepening and repetition of the death and rebirth. The prospect of physical death prompts this discovery.

Before proceeding to discussion of the fruits of a witness through death, it is appropriate to examine our own causes, both what they are now when death is certain and distant and what they might be if it were certain and near. The following simple questions pertain to our very complex living. You may be dissatisfied with the questions and your responses. It is almost impossible to indicate clearly what we are actually doing with our lives. But the attempt to contemplate our own "ultimate concerns" is a natural and useful response to the presence of death.

1. What are the three most significant causes in your life? Be brief. Do not state generalities or abstractions, but be as concrete and specific as possible.
   1. _____
   2. _____
   3. _____
2. How comprehensive are your causes?
   Cause 1   Very____   Somewhat____   Not____
   Cause 2   Very____   Somewhat____   Not____
   Cause 3   Very____   Somewhat____   Not____
3. How concrete are your causes?
   Cause 1   Very____   Somewhat____   Not____
   Cause 2   Very____   Somewhat____   Not____
   Cause 3   Very____   Somewhat____   Not____
4. How hopeful are your causes?
   Cause 1   Very____   Somewhat____   Not____
   Cause 2   Very____   Somewhat____   Not____
   Cause 3   Very____   Somewhat____   Not____
5. For which of your causes, if any, would you be willing to die? Imagine circumstances which would raise this issue for each cause.
   Cause 1   Willing____   Not Sure____   Unwilling____
   Cause 2   Willing____   Not Sure____   Unwilling____

Cause 3   Willing____   Not Sure____   Unwilling____

6. You have just been told that you have exactly one year to
   live. Now that you know you are dying, do your three most
   significant causes remain the same or do they differ? If
   they differ, indicate the new causes briefly and concretely.

   Cause 1   Same____   Differ_____

   Cause 2   Same____   Differ_____

   Cause 3   Same____   Differ_____

Consummation of Life

Martyrdom is being defined in this exercise as a witness
through death which consummates life. We tend to assume that
a witness through death involves great solemnity and even
greater suffering. This may be generally true, yet it need not be
so because martyrdom is a consummation of life. As Churchill
and his countrymen discovered, a consummated life is lived in a
time and place when and where it is "equally good to live or die."
Martyrdom is an adventure into paradise.

Consummation means at least two things: it means both the act
of *finishing* something and the act of *perfecting* something. In
the case of martyrdom, Karl Rahner defines it as both the end
and the perfection of life.[10] On this theme, a follower of Rahner
writes:

Death is a man's first completely personal act, and is, therefore, by
reason of its very being, the place above all others for the awakening
of consciousness, for freedom, for the encounter with God, for the final
decision about eternal destiny.[11]

Roman Catholic theologians lay a great deal of stress on the
moment of physical death. Perhaps they make more of death
than the martyrs themselves did!

Shakespeare wrote: "Cowards die many times before their
deaths; / The valiant never taste of death but once."[12] But
cowards are those who refuse to die and are always running

away from death, or the risks embodied in their idea of it. Yet they are the dead in life. The valiant are those who do die again and again, putting aside constant self-protection. So the early Christians who lived for the sake of Christ died many times during their lives. They died first when they heard the good news of the gospel—died to themselves and the world. And they died again and again throughout their lives, leaving selves behind, until that final death which coincided with physical death. What seems most momentous to us may not have been so to the martyrs. Nothing fundamentally new was involved in this last of a whole series of events. *They* focused on the cause for which they lived and died. *We* focus on the events of life and death that illuminate their cause. Our kind of praise of the martyr does him a disservice.

The suggestion is that we should separate the act of martyrdom from the event of physical death. If we focus on the cause rather than on the secondary matter of circumstances, then it can be affirmed that every full participation in what is for us a wholly valid cause is a finishing and perfecting of life. Physical death remains the final and greatest symbol for the act, but the potentiality for martyrdom is granted to every moment. So we need not wait for physical death through persecution or terminal illness, but ought really to die now, gestate now, and be reborn now. We can live now as a martyr lives—adventuring into paradise.

The issue of the time and place of paradise distinguishes a martyr from one who has no comprehensive, concrete, and life-consummating cause. As Piet Hein said in a "grook":

> Living is
>   a thing you do
> now or never—
>   which do you?[13]

The martyr is not anxious about his life and so remains oriented around the *here* and *now* of his existence. The nonmartyr is anxious about his life and so flees constantly to preoccupations about the *where* and *when,* the *there* and *then* of his existence. Anxiety makes the difference. Without anxiety, the present is the beginning of paradise. With anxiety, paradise must be at some other place, some other time.

It is probable that most of us are not living the life of martyrdom. We are like those existentialists who feel "thrown" into existence. We would not have this reaction to our lives if we saw ourselves as children of God, as children of nature, or even as true children of man. We are anxious because we see ourselves as born out of nothing—as our own cause. The present is consequently an occasion for panic, for elaborate planning, for flight to some other time and place. We try to protect ourselves by the consolation of *memories,* or *anticipations* of happier days. Unfortunately, our anxiety is as mobile as we are. The flight is never entirely successful. The elderly person who feels unwanted and unworthy may dwell in his memories of a time when he was highly regarded. Yet his past is never blameless and his present anxiety will help him uncover feelings of guilt for the mistakes and omissions in his life. The young person who feels unprepared and incapable may dwell in his visions of a time when he will be successful and acknowledged. Yet his future is unclear, and his present anxiety will help him uncover feelings of cowardice and failure. Flight from the present into some other time and place can momentarily dull our pain, but never remove it. As Paul Tillich points out in his sermon "The Eternal Now," the past and future are equally a blessing and a curse.[14] In the beginning there was the Garden of Eden *and* the fall of man; in the end there will be heaven *and* hell. Certainly memory and anticipation are great gifts, undoubtedly our finest means for survival. But sheer survival is not sufficient. Who wants to spend an entire lifetime simply coping with anxiety by planning for or looking back to some other time, some other place? Yet this is what we have done over and over again;

it is what we do now, and what we will probably do tomorrow and tomorrow.

A return from our retreat to the there and then is a return to the anxiety of the here and now. But it is also a return to the possibility of a cause which overcomes anxiety. For a cause touches the individual only in the present time and place. The anxiety of past, present, and future places can be transcended only in the present place, for a cause with which we can have live connection exists only in the present. A past and finished cause is dead, while a future cause is as yet unborn. We are not asked to serve yesterday or tomorrow. We are asked today, right now. It is acceptance of this demand in the midst of our present circumstances that destroys anxiety.

Of course we tend not to see it that way. It is not immediately apparent to us that witness destroys anxiety. So there are three possible responses to the demand: acceptance, perverted acceptance, and refusal. Each response understands martyrdom differently.

Acceptance of martyrdom implies that sacrifice is seen as the way of establishing and maintaining a relationship to the cause. What is given up is always oneself. This self is the old self, the one not connected to a cause—the anxious self. But when this is sacrificed, martyrdom is seen not as an act of suffering, but as release from suffering.

The other two understandings of martyrdom are quite different. The *perverted acceptance* of it involves sacrifice *as a defense* against anxiety rather than destroying it. The individual attempts to use a cause for his own sake, for the sake of his own anxious self. He will engage in what appears to be the additional suffering or sacrifice as a preventive measure for the future, hoping that he will ultimately gain new power to bolster his old self. This magical manipulation finally leads to an enormous increase of anxiety. The desire for more defenses leads to no defense.

The *refusal* of martyrdom implies that such sacrifice is simply more anxiety-provoking and to be avoided at all costs. The individual who refuses a cause suffers, and does not see himself in a position to increase his suffering. The fact that the cause is often presented to him as involving suffering reinforces his own personal understanding. Thus acceptance of martyrdom implies the understanding that anxiety is destroyed; perverted acceptance implies that more anxiety is taken on for the sake of future control over it; and refusal implies that more anxiety is intolerable. Only the martyr understands that love casts out anxiety.

To be a Christian martyr is to be discovered by God in our present places. He is always presenting himself to us, but we are usually looking elsewhere and do not meet him. To actually meet him is to live without anxiety in paradise. It is no longer to run back and forth to different times and places, but to find repose in the present. Our memories and anticipations are not destroyed, but they become servants rather than rulers of the present. Christ died not primarily for the sake of our pasts and futures, but for the sake of our lives right now. The New Testament is filled with a sense of urgency which cannot be removed by demythologization. "Fool! This night your soul is required of you. . . ." "Repent, for the kingdom of God is at hand." The time and place in which paradise is at hand is always the here and now. To stop running to the there and then, to face the anxiety of the present place and then accept the cause that destroys anxiety—this is to live the life of a martyr. And it is the martyr who actually lives in paradise. His life proclaims: paradise is either here and now or it is nowhere and never!

What would it be like to become unbound from the anxiety of the here and now and from defensive running to the there and then? What would it be like to live in our present places in the presence of God? In other words, what would it be like to be alive?[15]

Paradise is the time and place for adventures. According to the dictionary, the noun "adventure" refers to happenings that occur by chance, involve risk, and are striking or remarkable in nature. These three elements are a part of any child's playful adventure. From the conscious point of view, his play suddenly happens by chance. Its occurrence is an occasion for surprise and wonder. The adventures of King Arthur's knights, the adventures of Sherlock Holmes, and the adventures of small boys all reveal the thrill of the unexpected. The factors of risk, hazard, and danger are equally apparent. These are the sources of the basic suspense of play where there is no predictable outcome. Whether the contest is with oneself, as in learning to spin a top; with others, as in the game of soccer; or with nature, as in the climbing of a mountain, the results are uncertain and the play is challenging. And it is important to note that success is not an issue. As countless observers have pointed out, what is crucial is to play the game and be a "good sport." The kite may be caught and torn by the branches of a tree; in a formal contest one side always loses (or nearly always, ties being a rarity); and in climbing a mountain, a life may be lost. The adventurer knows this full well. His trust is not in the naïve promise of a successful outcome, but in the value of the adventure for its own sake. Finally, the phenomenon of play adventure is deemed remarkable by the participant. The player never loses consciousness of the fact that he is playing, always remaining aware of the differences between the world of play and the world of every day. If this were not so, there could be no attitude of adventure, no sense of an unusual and different experience. The adventurer is in this world, but in a different way than usual; he is not quite *of* this world. To have an adventure is to participate in happenings which take place by chance, entail risk, and are of remarkable purport.

There have been moments in all our lives when we have been surprised into adventures. At various times and places we have been carried beyond our usual need for protection, have been precipitated into spontaneity and trust in whatever happened. We were not particularly concerned about success or failure—

life or death. Just living in the adventure was sufficient. For a while a story was being told by our actions. And when the adventure was over, we spoke of it to our friends with some hyperbole.

These adventures have occurred many times during our development. As infants we had adventures when we discovered our toes for the first time and when we experimented with gravity by dropping spoons to the floor from the height of our high chair. As children we saw giants and wild beasts on the way home from school and told our mothers about them. As juveniles we played house and nurse, cowboys and Indians, and dug caves or built tree houses in the manner of primitives. As adolescents we were often confused and troubled, but sometimes surprised into adventures with sex, vocation, and philosophy of life. We remember our first date and our first kiss. We remember many times and places when there were surprises. We are grateful for them. And we enjoy the children and youth of our world precisely because they have such adventures.

But our nostalgia and delight in the young remind us that we do not have so many adventures as mature adults. And when we do have them, they are not in fact so very mature. Usually our rare adventures would be more appropriate for someone at an earlier stage of development. We race cars or sailboats, play touch football or bridge, read novels or attend plays. Only if we are quite fortunate is our marriage or vocation an adventure at times.

But what if we were surprised into a fully mature adventure which encompassed our total existence? This adventure, however similar to all the little adventures we have known, would be of so much greater depth and breadth as to *seem* entirely different. If this actually happened to us, we would call it "holy." And we would respond with unparalleled hyperbole in feeling, in thought, and in daily living. Like Moses before the burning bush, we would take off our shoes and kneel on holy ground; like David before the ark of God, we would kick up our heels with delight. It is because such mature adventures have occurred that every culture tells the tallest of tall tales, which are myths, and plays the most far-out games, which are rituals. Religion is created by the adventures of mature human beings at play.

Since we have all had little adventures, we have some awareness of what a big adventure would be like. Four elements predominate: peace, delight, freedom, and unworldliness.

The adventurer has a sense of peace. This is not the peace of inaction which stems from the anxiety of the old self. Our anxiety leads to an apparent peace which is really a stalemate, a condition of shock and immobility. The peace of the adventurer lies rather in action. There is an ease and contentment with what is going on which does not inhibit action but fosters it. The activity of the adventurer is like that of an athlete who no longer has to work and worry over moving his body correctly. He is always on the move in a peaceful way.

The adventurer also has a sense of delight. He is a dilettante in the original sense of the term; that is, one who takes delight in something. This delight is different from what we mean by pleasure. Pleasure and pain belong together in the world of anxiety. They are a result of achieving and failing to achieve defense against anxiety. But the adventurer does not have to work at this task. Such anxiety as remains is ruled over by delight. There is danger in the adventurer's fun, fear in his joy, and awe in his rapture. Yet these are welcomed as a necessary part of the adventure. Even our suffering becomes an occasion for wonder and delight. To delight in happenings is to put suffering in its proper place.

Along with peace and delight, the adventurer has a sense of freedom. Think of all the kinds of freedom manifest in the adventures we have had. There may be a sense of bodily freedom, as in children's frolic and acrobatics, where the skip and the somersault defy gravity. There is the experience of freedom from ordinary time, as when children play kick-the-can and are oblivious to the supposed demands of past and future. There is freedom over causality and destiny, for all adventurers possess equal chances in their games and equal opportunities to play a role in a drama. There is freedom of the emotions and intellect, for the player may freely show many negative emotions which do not harm him or his playmates, and he need have no concern to use his mind for the creation of useful products for survival. And there is a sense of freedom from everyday social reality, for we are free to be ourselves just as we are and to be ourselves just as we are with others. The freedom of the adventurer is that freedom from anxiety which grants both freedom *from* denial of what is happening and freedom *for* complete participation in it.

Finally, the adventurer has a sense of unworldliness. He is not out of this world like the insane who have been overcome by anxiety, but neither is he in the world like the sane who have been overcome by their defenses. Whereas the insane have lost the old self and the normal are caught by it, the adventurer has discovered something new. He is charmed and fascinated by a new vision of the world and of himself. And he shares this vision with all who encounter him. He is not of this world, but he is surely in it. His excitement is contagious and others may be swept up into the adventure with him. Even our parents were sometimes caught by the wild tales we told them as children. They were not always spoilsports, but were brought to life by our adventures. So the mature adventurer is one who lives and tells a story. Just as the child says, "I'm a cowboy," the mature adult may say, "I'm a child of God." And the story being told is accepted as complete in itself. It is not shrouded with dogma and creed. It is not besieged by such questions as "Is the story true?" "Is there only one story?" or "Who made the story up?" It is not lived or told to convince or convert someone to a particular point of view or to suggest a specific action. If such things occur, the story has fallen into the hands of the everyday anxious world and is no longer a true tale of adventure. To actually participate in an adventure abolishes all need to justify it to oneself or others. Adventures occur only in paradise and paradise requires no defense.

This understanding of paradise may seem irrelevant and irreverent. That is, it is silent about things that are of weighty concern to man. Not to mention the suffering of others seems to imply irrelevance to this life. And not to mention life after death seems to imply irreverence to God. But we ought to have some caution about these judgments because martyrs have sometimes seemed irrelevant and irreverent. It could be that the weighty concerns which preoccupy us are precisely the concerns that drag us down to hell. The fault lies not so much with the concerns as with their source: our anxiety. The martyr is not anxious. Therefore he is free to love other human beings. Love is that act which reveals delight in change; which occurs because of a cause which is comprehensive, concrete, and hopeful; and which accomplishes, over and over again, that completion and perfection which is consummation. The martyr is the one who can fully participate in another's suffering. And he participates by showing the possibility of a new life. We, on the other hand, are not free from anxiety and so participate in the suffering of others only because it reminds us of our own suffering and helps us control it. Our relevance to the world is a defense against anxiety. And because the martyr is not anxious, he is free to live in this world and not worry about other worlds. For him this is God's world and that is sufficient for one's adventures. And we who are always on the run? Perhaps our concern about life after death is a defense against anxiety and so an irreverence toward God. When *we* are silent about suffering and death, we are probably irrelevant and irreverent. But the silence of the martyr may be of another kind—the silence of a man in Christ.

> Follow Him thrrough the land of Unlikeness:
> You will see rare beasts and have unique adventures.[16]

How are we to be reborn? Through that most powerful manifestation of love which is martyrdom. We are to accept a cause which will lead us to a witness through death which consummates life. When and if this happens to us, we will experience the joy of martyrdom. You have already reflected on the three most significant causes in your life. And you have considered the extent to which you would be willing to die for these causes. One final question remains. You have answered it before in the exercise on fear. Do so again. If you can answer it affirmatively, be grateful for the gift you have received. If you cannot answer it, have mercy on yourself; keep asking the question, and the gift of an answer will come eventually.

1. Under what conditions, if any, would you be able to accept your having to die as a *joyful* conclusion to your life. Be brief. Be concrete.

Wonder

"In the midst of life we are in death," and "Death is a truth made profound by the size of our wonder." So we have wondered about our own death. We have wondered about our own denial, fear, death in life, grief, belief, and martyrdom. Hopefully we have wondered sufficiently to engender the process of death, gestation, and rebirth. If so, we have discovered life in the midst of death.

It has not been the intent of these exercises to prepare us for either a "dignified" death or a "dignified" life. The purpose has been to increase our wonder about death and life. Adventures are wonderful, but not necessarily dignified. They are full of surprises. And surprises usually make a fuss. Those who really wonder make a great fuss in their living and dying. The danger is that our wonder will diminish. G. K. Chesterton has discovered:

This at least seems to be the main problem for philosophers. . . . How can we contrive to be at once astonished at the world and yet at home in it? How can this world give us at once the fascination of a strange town and the comfort and honour of being our own town? We need this life of practical romance; the combination of something that is strange with something that is secure. We need to view the world so as to combine an idea of wonder and an idea of welcome. We need to be happy in this wonderland without once being merely comfortable. . . .[17]

No life without wonder and no wonder without welcome. So the mystery of death must remain. It is not a puzzle to be solved, any more than is life. And the welcome that wonder needs is the product of love. It has been reported that when Goethe was about to die, he cried, "Light, the world needs more light." Years later, someone responded: "No, Goethe was wrong, what he should have said was 'Warmth, the world needs more warmth.' We shall not die from the dark, but from the cold."[18] The mystery of death remains and is matched by the mystery of love.

After reviewing all that they have done in response to these exercises, participants have wondered again. They have said:

Death—the great leveller. I grow weary of him. Yet I still fear him, or is it life I fear? I'm kind of grateful for death—without him life would have little meaning. Yet I also think he is a bastard. Ambivalent? You're damned right!

Contemplating "my own death" at this point is not quite the game of silence it was for me six weeks ago. The major difference is that six weeks ago I really thought about death and what it would mean for me to *die;* tonight, when I contemplate my death, I am driven to look at my *life* and what it means to *live now.*

I am fully aware that I will die, and that in some ways I am dying now. I look forward to the event, because I am curious about how I will feel when it happens, and if there will be anything at all on the other side. I accept the fact of my death as an integral part of my having lived.

I can say I have fully come to terms with my death. I can also walk on water and fly like a bird.

I can only *wonder* what to say, for I can only *wonder* at death. What do I *know?* Only that I must *live* responsibly and lovingly.

Our own exercise in dying and living is never finished. These formal exercises can be concluded, but not by any suitable quotation, by my own thoughts, or even by statements from participants. Only you can provide the conclusion. So review and reflect on your own statements, drawings, and answers to questions. As you did in the beginning, write fifty words of wonder about your own death. Hopefully, you have been surprised by yourself many times during each exercise. May you always be surprised by your own dying and living.

NOTES

EXERCISE 1: IN THE MIDST OF LIFE

1. Marc Golden, quoted by Sam Blum in "Who Decides What Gets on TV—and Why," *New York Times Magazine*, September 3, 1967.

2. Geoffrey Gorer, "The Pornography of Death," *Death, Grief, and Mourning* (New York: Doubleday & Co., 1967), pp. 192–99.

3. Franz Borkenau, "The Concept of Death," in *Death and Identity*, ed. Robert Fulton (New York: John Wiley & Sons, 1965), pp. 42–56.

4. Barney G. Glaser and Anselm L. Strauss, *Awareness of Dying* (Chicago: Aldine Publishing Co., 1966), pp. 132 ff.

5. August M. Kasper, "The Doctor and Death," in *The Meaning of Death*, ed. Herman Feifel (New York: McGraw-Hill Book Co., 1959), p. 266.

6. Sigmund Freud, "Thoughts for the Times on War and Death," in *On War, Sex and Neurosis* (New York: Arts & Sciences Press, 1947), p. 263.

7. Glaser and Strauss, *op. cit.*

8. John Gunther, *Death Be Not Proud: A Memoir* (New York: Pyramid Books, 1963).

9. This telling of an old tale is adapted from a version by W.

Somerset Maugham in his play *Sheppy* (New York: Doubleday & Co., 1934).

EXERCISE 2: FEAR OF DEATH AND LIFE

1. William Shakespeare, *Measure for Measure*, Act III, Scene 1.

2. James Boswell, *The Life of Samuel Johnson* (New York: E. P. Dutton & Co., 1931), 2: 212–13.

3. C. G. Jung, *Memories, Dreams, Reflections* (New York: Random House, 1961), pp. 289–91.

4. Leo Tolstoy, "The Death of Ivan Ilych," *The Death of Ivan Ilych and Other Stories* (New York: Signet Classic, 1964), pp. 125, 129–30, 155–56.

5. Walt Whitman, "When Lilacs Last in the Doorway Bloom'd," *The Poetry and Prose of Walt Whitman* (New York: Simon & Schuster, 1949), p. 323.

6. Arnold Toynbee, "The Relation Between Life and Death, Living and Dying," in *Man's Concern with Death*, Arnold Toynbee and Others (New York: McGraw-Hill Book Co. 1968), p. 271.

7. For these categories, I am indebted to Jacques Choron, *Modern Man and Mortality* (New York: The Macmillan Co., 1964), pp. 73–83.

8. Corliss Lamont, *The Illusion of Immortality*, 2d ed. (New York: Philosophical Library, 1950), p. 222.

9. G. Stanley Hall, quoted by Choron *op. cit.*, p. 79.

10. John Fowles, *The Magus* (New York: Little, Brown & Co., 1965), pp. 500–502.

EXERCISE 3: DEATH IN LIFE

1. Michelangelo, quoted by William I. Langer in "The Black Death," *Scientific American* 210 (February 1964): 121.

2. Saul Bellow, *Herzog* (New York: Viking Press, 1964), pp. 289–90.

3. Albert Camus, *The Myth of Sisyphus and Other Essays*, trans. J. O'Brien (New York: Alfred A. Knopf, 1955), p. 21.

4. Dorothy Parker, "Resume," *The Collected Works of Dorothy Parker* (New York: Viking Press, 1936), p. 50.

5. Søren Kierkegaard, "The Sickness unto Death," *Fear and Trembling and the Sickness unto Death* (Garden City, N.Y.: Doubleday & Co., 1954), p. 151.

6. Albert Camus, "The Wrong Side and the Right Side," *Lyrical and Critical Essays*, ed. Philip Thody, trans. Ellen Conroy Kennedy (New York: Vintage Books, 1970), pp. 58–59, 61.

7. Charles William Wahl, "Suicide as a Magical Act," in *Clues to Suicide*, ed. Edwin S. Shneidman and Norman L. Farberow (New York: McGraw-Hill Book Co., 1957), pp. 22–30.

8. Herbert Hendin, *Suicide and Scandinavia* (Garden City, N.Y.: Doubleday & Co., 1965), pp. 21–30.

9. The following discussion is indebted to a provocative essay by James Hillman, *Suicide and the Soul* (New York: Harper & Row, 1964).

10. Karl Menninger, *Man Against Himself* (New York: Harcourt, Brace & World, 1938), p. 23.

11. *Ibid.*, p. 44.

12. *Ibid.*, pp. 23–24.

13. Don D. Jackson, "Theories of Suicide, in Shneidman and Farberow, *op. cit.*, p. 17.

14. Hillman, *op. cit.*, p. 81.

15. *Ibid.*, pp. 88–89.

16. Herman Melville, *Moby Dick* (New York: Modern Library, 1930), p. 1.

EXERCISE 4: TRANSFORMATION BY GRIEF

1. Anton Chekov, quoted by Lionel Trilling in *The Experience of Literature* (Garden City, N.Y.: Doubleday & Co., 1967), p. 550.

2. Erich Lindemann, "Symptomatology and Management of

Acute Grief," *American Journal of Psychiatry* 101 (1944): 141–48, reprinted in Fulton, ed., *Death and Identity*, pp. 186–201.

3. Edna St. Vincent Millay, "Lament," *Second April* (New York: Mitchell Kennerley, 1921), pp. 64–65.

4. Barney G. Glaser and Anselm L. Strauss, *Time for Dying* (Chicago: Aldine Publishing Co., 1968), p. 7.

5. Ambrose Bierce, "The Devoted Widow," in *The Collected Writings of Ambrose Bierce* (New York: Citadel Press, 1947), p. 576.

6. Rainer Maria Rilke, *The Notebooks of Malte Laurids Brigge*, trans. M. D. Herter (New York: W. W. Norton & Co., 1949), pp. 17–18.

7. Elisabeth Kubler-Ross, *On Death and Dying* (New York: The Macmillan Co., 1969).

8. Avery D. Weisman and Thomas P. Hackett, *"Predilection to Death,"* *Psychosomatic Medicine* 23 (1961), reprinted in Fulton, ed., *Death and Identity*, p. 324.

9. Lael Tucker Wertenbaker, *Death of a Man* (New York: Random House, 1957).

10. C. Knight Aldrich, "The Dying Patient's Grief," *Jama* 184 (May 4, 1963): 329, 330.

11. Mircea Eliade, *Rites and Symbols of Initiation: The Mysteries of Birth and Rebirth*, trans. Willard R. Trask (New York: Harper Torchbooks, 1965), pp. 21–40.

EXERCISE 5: LIFE IN DEATH

1. Thornton Wilder, *Our Town* (New York: Harper & Row, 1963), p. 81.

2. André Malraux, *Man's Fate*, trans. Haakon M. Chevalier (New York: Vintage Books, 1961), pp. 337–38.

3. The following discussion is indebted to the study of Edgar Herzog, *Psyche and Death* (New York: G. P. Putnam's Sons, for the C. G. Jung Foundation for Analytical Psychology, 1967).

4. Maria H. Nagy, "The Child's View of Death," *Journal of*

Genetic Psychology 73: 3–27 (1948); reprinted in Feifel, ed., *The Meaning of Death*, pp. 79–98.

5. For discussion of these specific beliefs see Liston O. Mills, ed., *Perspectives on Death* (Nashville: Abingdon Press, 1969) and Milton McC. Gatch, *Death: Meaning and Mortality in Christian Thought and Contemporary Culture* (New York: Seabury Press, 1969).

6. David C. McClelland, "The Harlequin Complex," *The Study of Lives*, ed. Robert W. White (New York: Atherton Press, 1963), pp. 107–119.

7. Albert Camus, *The Stranger*, trans. Stuart Gilbert (New York: Vintage Books, 1946), pp. 149–50.

8. Albert Camus, *The Plague*, trans. Stuart Gilbert (Harmondsworth, Middlesex, England: Penguin Books, 1967), pp. 244–45, 251–52.

9. Gatch, *op. cit.*, pp. 180–81.

10. *Ibid.*, pp. 184–85.

EXERCISE 6: IN THE MIDST OF DEATH

1. Ivan Turgenev, "The Sparrow," trans. Constance Garnett, in Barry Ulanov, comp., *Death: A Book of Preparation and Consolation* (New York: Sheed & Ward, 1959), pp. 107–108.

2. Tertullian, quoted by Karl Menninger in *Man Against Himself* (New York: Harcourt, Brace & World, 1938), p. 79.

3. Ignatius, quoted in Menninger, *op. cit.*, pp. 124–25.

4. Karl Rahner, "On Martyrdom," *On the Theology of Death* (New York: Herder & Herder, 1964), pp. 89–127.

5. *Ibid.*, p. 95.

6. Last words of John Wilkes Booth, April 26, 1865, *Dictionary of American Biography*, quoted in *The American Treasury: 1455-1955* (New York: Harper & Brothers, 1955), p. 464.

7. K. R. Eissler, *The Psychiatrist and the Dying Patient* (New York: International Universities Press, 1955), p. 126.

8. Rahner, *op. cit.*, p. 105.

9. John Gunther, *Death Be Not Proud: A Memoir* (New York: Pyramid Books, 1963), p. 192.

10. Rahner, *op. cit.,*

11. Ladislaus Boros, *The Mystery of Death* (New York: Herder & Herder, 1965), p. 84.

12. William Shakespeare, *Julius Caesar,* Act II, Scene 2.

13. Piet Hein, "Living Is," in *Grooks* (Garden City, N.Y.: Doubleday & Co., 1969), p. 53.

14. Paul Tillich, "The Eternal Now," in Feifel, ed., *The Meaning of Death,* pp. 30–38.

15. For full discussion of the elements of adventure, see my earlier work, *In Praise of Play: Toward a Psychology of Religion* (New York: Harper & Row, 1969).

16. W. H. Auden, "For the Time Being," *The Collected Poetry of W. H. Auden* (New York: Random House, 1945), p. 466.

17. G. K. Chesterton, *Orthodoxy* (London: Bodley Head, 1949), p. 4.

18. This story was told by one of the early participants in these exercises, Timothy Buxton. The source is unknown.

SELECTED BIBLIOGRAPHY

EXERCISE 1: IN THE MIDST OF LIFE

Bierce, Ambrose. "An Occurrence at Owl Creek Bridge." In *In the Midst of Life and Other Stories.* New York: Signet Books, 1961. (Paperback)

This short story is a striking and moving example of denial in the immediate presence of death.

Borkenau, Franz. "The Concept of Death." In *Death and Identity,* edited by Robert Fulton. New York: John Wiley & Sons, 1965.

A volume which will be repeatedly suggested in this bibliography. The article by Borkenau considers cultures which are death-accepting, death-defying, or death-denying.

Geis, Gilbert, and Fulton, Robert. "Death and Social Values." In *Death and Identity.*

A general statement on death as a taboo subject with an interesting conclusion on the dilemma of a funeral director who is called upon both to blunt and to sharpen the reality of death.

Glaser, Barney G., and Strauss, Anselm L. *Awareness of Dying.* Chicago: Aldine Publishing Co., 1966.

A discussion of awareness contexts in the dying situation. The problems and possibilities for the patient, relatives, and hospital staff are presented in the contexts of closed awareness, suspicion awareness, mutual pretense, and open awareness.

Gorer, Geoffrey. "The Pornography of Death." *Death, Grief, and Mourn-*

ing. Garden City, N.Y.: Doubleday & Co., 1967. (Paperback)

The short, classic essay on the theme of death, rather than sex, being pornographic for our society.

Kasper, August M. "The Doctor and Death." In *The Meaning of Death,* edited by Herman Feifel. New York: McGraw-Hill Book Co., 1959. (Paperback)

A volume which will be repeatedly recommended in this bibliography. The article by Kasper is a review of the doctor's difficulties in work with the dying.

Parsons, Talcott, and Lidz, Victor. "Death in American Society." In *Essays in Self-Destruction,* edited by Edwin S. Shneidman. New York: Science House, 1967.

A sociological examination of the hypothesis that American society's orientation to death is "not a 'denial' " but a mode of acceptance appropriate to our primary cultural patterns of activism.

Waugh, Evelyn. *The Loved One.* New York: Dell Publishing Co., 1954. (Paperback)

A comic account of the euphemistic approach to death, based on the practices of Forest Lawn Memorial Park in California.

EXERCISE 2: FEAR OF DEATH AND LIFE

Chadwick, Mary. "Notes upon the Fear of Death." In *Death: Interpretations,* edited by Henrik M. Ruitenbeek. New York: Delta Book, 1969. (Paperback)

A Freudian analysis of anxiety over death in children.

Choron, Jacques. *Modern Man and Mortality.* New York: The Macmillan Co., 1964.

Chapters 4–12 consider the fear of death and related responses from philosophical and psychological perspectives.

Fulton, Robert, ed. *Death and Identity.* New York: John Wiley & Sons, 1965.

Part II of this volume consists of essays on attitudes and responses to death. Most of the content is on fear. Results of reported research are often contradictory. These essays suggest both the variety of human responses and our lack of knowledge about them.

Tillich, Paul. *The Courage to Be.* New Haven: Yale University Press, 1952. (Paperback)

Chapters 2 and 3 explore types of anxiety and pathological anxiety from philosophical and theological perspectives. The anxiety of fate and death is considered to be the "most basic, most universal, and inescapable."

Tolstoy, Leo. "The Death of Ivan Ilych." *The Death of Ivan Ilych and Other Stories.* New York: Signet Classic, 1964. (Paperback)

The classic story on death. A superb portrayal of denial, fear, and grief.

Wahl, Charles W. "The Fear of Death." In both *The Meaning of Death* and *Death and Identity.*

A psychological examination of the fear of death in children as a composite of mutually contradictory paradoxes.

EXERCISE 3: DEATH IN LIFE

Hillman, James. *Suicide and the Soul.* New York: Harper & Row, 1964.

An unusual and provocative theory of suicide from a Jungian perspective.

Jackson, Don D. "Theories of Suicide." In *Clues to Suicide,* edited by Edwin S. Shneidman and Norman L. Farberow. New York: McGraw-Hill Book Co., 1957. (Paperback)

A concise review of the theories of Freud, Durkheim, and other psychoanalytic and socioeconomic theories.

Kierkegaard, Søren. "The Sickness unto Death." In *Fear and Trembling and The Sickness unto Death.* Translated by Walter Lowrie. Garden City, N.Y.: Doubleday & Co., 1954. (Paperback)

A philosophical analysis of despair. Of special pertinence is the understanding of it as "the disconsolateness of not being able to die."

Levin, Tom. "Leave It to George." *Invitation to a Dark Room.* New York: Macfadden Book, 1964. (Paperback)

A psychoanalyst reports his encounter with a patient who eventually commits suicide.

Plath, Sylvia. *The Bell Jar.* New York: Bantam Books, 1972. (Paperback)

An autobiographical novel of attempted suicide by a gifted poetess who later committed suicide.

Shneidman, Edwin S. "Orientations Toward Death." *The Psychology of Suicide.* New York: Science House, 1970.

Classification of the role of the individual in his own death as intentioned, subintentioned, or unintentioned. A "psychological autopsy" of Melville's Captain Ahab is used to illustrate these concepts.

Wahl, Charles William. "Suicide as a Magical Act." In *Clues to Suicide.*

A psychoanalytic discussion of motivations for suicide which perceives it as a magical act occurring for the sake of illusory ends.

Weisman, Avery D., and Hackett, Thomas P. "Predilection to Death." In *Death and Identity.*

This essay contains valuable case material and theory on many aspects of death. It includes discussion of patients who are convinced of approaching death and regard it as appropriate.

EXERCISE 4: TRANSFORMATION BY GRIEF

Agee, James. *A Death in the Family.* New York: Avon Publications, 1957. (Paperback)

A major novel which portrays the grief of family and relatives over the death of a man. The atmosphere is both nostalgic and realistic.

de Beauvoir, Simone. *A Very Easy Death.* New York: G. P. Putnam's Sons, 1966.

The title is ironic. The author describes her experience of the death of her mother.

Eliade, Mircea. *Rites and Symbols of Initiation: The Mysteries of Birth and*

Rebirth. Translated by Willard R. Trask. New York: Harper Torch-books, 1965. (Paperback)

An examination of patterns of initiation in traditional societies with emphasis on the dynamics of annihilation and rebirth. This is a useful introduction to an understanding of initiatory grief.

Kubler-Ross, Elisabeth. *On Death and Dying.* New York: The Macmilllan Co., 1969. (Paperback)

Clinical discussion of the stages of denial, anger, bargaining, depression, acceptance, and hope in the dying patient. A very concrete and practical treatment of what the dying have to teach the living.

Lindemann, Erich. "Symptomatology and Management of Acute Grief." In *Death and Identity*.

This is the classic study of the grief process which presents basic theory and analysis of the reactions of the bereaved survivors of victims of the Cocoanut Grove fire.

Mandelbaum, David G. "Social Uses of Funeral Rites." In both *The Meaning of Death* and *Death and Identity*.

A consideration of rites in many cultures and discussion of such purposes of the funeral as disposal of the body, aiding the bereaved to reorient themselves, and asserting the viability of society.

Volkart, Edmund H., and Michael, Stanley T., "Bereavement and Mental Health." In *Death and Identity*.

Presents cultural perspectives on grief and is especially useful in its treatment of problems in American society.

Wertenbaker, Lael Tucker. *Death of a Man.* New York: Random House, 1957.

A woman's account of the dying and death of her husband.

EXERCISE 5: LIFE IN DEATH

Camus, Albert. *The Plague.* Translated by Stuart Gilbert. Harmonds-worth, Middlesex, England: Penguin Books, 1967. (Paperback)

A novel of the twentieth-century experience of death in which meaning is found through enduring, loving, and healing.

Gatch, Milton McC. *Death: Meaning and Morality in Christian Thought and Contemporary Culture.* New York: Seabury Press, 1969.

A survey of concepts and beliefs concerning death which begins with classical Greek and Old Testament times, proceeds through to the time of the Reformation, and concludes with a contemporary interpretation of beliefs in immortality and resurrection.

Gottlieb, Carla. "Modern Art and Death." In *The Meaning of Death.*

An historical approach to images of death in art which reveals the great variety of images and suggests possible implications of leading contemporary ones.

Herzog, Edgar. *Psyche and Death.* New York: G. P. Putnam's Sons for the C. G. Jung Foundation for Analytical Psychology, 1967.

The first part of this work is a review of primitive images of death. The second part is an analysis of contemporary dreams of death. A Jungian statement on the relation of death and psychic transformation.

Hoffman, Frederick J. "Mortality and Modern Literature." In *The Meaning of Death.*

A discussion of the relation of death to grace, violence, and self in modern man. The hypothesis is that "the violent destruction of the possibilities of grace has forced upon the self the responsibility of adjustment to death."

Nagy, Maria H. "The Child's View of Death." In *The Meaning of Death.*

A report of research on children's attitudes toward death that includes much concrete data and a useful developmental framework.

Stendahl, Krister, ed. *Immortality and Resurrection.* New York: The Macmillan Co., 1965. (Paperback)

This volume contains Oscar Cullmann's very useful essay on the contrast between the deaths of Socrates and Jesus and on the distinctions between immortality and resurrection. Three additional essays also consider the tension between these two basic concepts.

Toynbee, Arnold. "Traditional Attitudes Toward Death." In *Man's Con-*

cern with Death, edited by Arnold Toynbee and others. New York: McGraw-Hill Book Co., 1969.

This volume contains many essays on beliefs about death. The essay by Toynbee is a broad survey.

EXERCISE 6: IN THE MIDST OF DEATH

Gollwitzer, Helmut; Kuhn, Kathe and Schneider, Reinhold, eds. *Dying We Live.* New York: Pantheon Books, 1956.

An extraordinary collection of farewell letters written in the face of death by men and women of the German resistance during World War II. Unquestionable testimony on the presence of life in the midst of death.

Gunther, John. *Death Be Not Proud: A Memoir.* New York: Pyramid Books, 1963. (Paperback)

This is the story of the death of John Gunther's adolescent son. Even though his death could not be avoided, this is a memoir of martyrdom.

Neale, Robert E. *In Praise of Play: Toward a Psychology of Religion.* New York: Harper & Row, Publishers, 1969.

A psychological study of play and of religion as play. Contains a phenomenological description of the quality of life that occurs when anxiety over survival is absent.

Rahner, Karl. *On the Theology of Death.* New York: Herder & Herder, 1964. (Paperback)

This volume consists of two essays on death and dying from the Roman Catholic perspective. The longer essay includes a section on death as a dying with Christ. The shorter essay is on martyrdom itself. Both essays can be quite stimulating to Protestants and humanists.

Tillich, Paul. "The Eternal Now." In *The Meaning of Death.*

A sermon on the mysteries of time and destiny, which focuses on the possibility of resting in the present.

Tillich, Paul. *The Courage to Be.* New Haven: Yale University Press, 1952. (Paperback)

Courage is defined as "the readiness to take upon oneself negatives, anticipated by fear, for the sake of a fuller positivity." Chapters 4, 5, and 6 explore the courage to be as a part, the courage to be as oneself, and the courage to accept acceptance.

73 74 10 9 8 7 6 5 4 3 2 1